PROBABILITY CONCEPTS

NCEA Level 3 External

Charlotte Walker and Victoria Walker

Walker Maths 3.13 Probability Concepts
1st Edition
Charlotte Walker
Victoria Walker

Editor: Eva Chan
Cover and text designer: Cheryl Smith, Macarn Design
Production controller: Siew Han Ong
Reprint: Alice Kane

Any URLs contained in this publication were checked for currency during the production process. Note, however, that the publisher cannot vouch for the ongoing currency of URLs.

Acknowledgements
Cover photo courtesy of Shutterstock.

We wish to thank the Boards of Trustees of Darfield and Riccarton High Schools for allowing us to use materials and ideas developed while teaching. Our thanks also go to all past and present colleagues who have generously shared their expertise and ideas.

© 2016 Cengage Learning Australia Pty Limited

Copyright Notice
Copyright: This book is not a photocopiable master. This book is sold on the basis that it will be used by an individual teacher or student. No part of the publication may be copied, stored or communicated in any form by any means (paper or digital), including recording or storing in an electronic retrieval system, without the written permission of the publisher. Copying permitted under licence to Copyright Licensing New Zealand does not extend to any copying from this book.

For product information and technology assistance,
in Australia call **1300 790 853**;
in New Zealand call **0800 449 725**

For permission to use material from this text or product, please email **aust.permissions@cengage.com**

National Library of New Zealand Cataloguing-in-Publication Data
A catalogue record for this book is available from the National Library of New Zealand.

978 0 17 038937 2

Cengage Learning Australia
Level 7, 80 Dorcas Street
South Melbourne, Victoria Australia 3205

Cengage Learning New Zealand
Unit 4B Rosedale Office Park
331 Rosedale Road, Albany, North Shore 0632, NZ

For learning solutions, visit **cengage.co.nz**

Printed in China by 1010 Printing International Limited
17 27 26 25

CONTENTS

Formulae 4

Glossary 4

The language of probability 6

Probability revision 9

True probability, experimental probability and theoretical (model) probability 13

Multiplication Principle 14

Methods for displaying probability 17
- Probability and frequency distribution tables and graphs 17
- Venn diagrams and probability tables 21
- Probabilities with two overlapping groups 22
- Probabilities with three overlapping groups 28
- Probabilities from tables of counts 36
- Probability trees 40

Interrelationships between events 49
- Mutually exclusive (disjoint) events 49
- Events that are not mutually exclusive 50

Removable section in the centre of the book. Pull out and cut up.

- Complementary events (A and A') 51
- Conditional probability 52
- Putting it together 55
- Independent events 59

Risk 65

Sampling and randomness 73
- Sampling 73
- Randomness 74

Simulation 75

Practice questions 81

Answers 87

ISBN: 9780170389372 PHOTOCOPYING OF THIS PAGE IS RESTRICTED UNDER LAW.

Formulae

These are the formulae that will be supplied to you in the external examination.

Permutations and combinations	${}^{n}P_{r} = \frac{n!}{(n-r)!}$ $\binom{n}{r} = {}^{n}C_{r} = \frac{n!}{(n-r)!r!}$
Probability	$P(A \cup B) = P(A) + P(B) - P(A \cap B)$ $P(A \mid B) = \frac{P(A \cap B)}{P(B)}$

Glossary

Make your own glossary of key terms:

Term	Definition	Picture/Example
Factorial		
Multiplication Principle		
And		
Or		
Either		
Between		

PHOTOCOPYING OF THIS PAGE IS RESTRICTED UNDER LAW.
ISBN: 9780170389372

Term	Definition	Picture/Example
Independent		
Intersection		
Union		
Complementary events		
Mutually exclusive events		
Absolute risk		
Relative risk		
True probability		
Experimental probability		
Theoretical probability		
Venn diagram		
Inference		
Bias		
Random		
Simulation		

ISBN: 9780170389372 PHOTOCOPYING OF THIS PAGE IS RESTRICTED UNDER LAW.

The language of probability

You need to understand the notation and words used in probability.

Let X be a **discrete** variable that can take values between 0 and 8.

Notation

Notation	The values that X can take are highlighted:	This could also be written as:
$P(X = 3)$	0 1 2 **3** 4 5 6 7 8	$P(2 < X < 4)$
$P(X > 3)$	0 1 2 3 **4 5 6 7 8**	$P(X \geq 4)$
$P(X < 3)$	**0 1 2** 3 4 5 6 7 8	$P(X \leq 2)$
$P(X \geq 3)$	0 1 2 **3 4 5 6 7 8**	$P(X > 2)$
$P(X \leq 3)$	**0 1 2 3** 4 5 6 7 8	$P(X < 4)$
$P(2 < X < 7)$	0 1 2 **3 4 5 6** 7 8	$P(3 \leq X \leq 6)$
$P(2 \leq X \leq 7)$	0 1 **2 3 4 5 6 7** 8	$P(1 < X < 8)$

Complete the table.

Notation	Highlight the numbers included in the description in the left column:	This could also be written as:
$P(X > 3)$	0 1 2 3 4 5 6 7 8	$P(X \geq \quad)$
$P(X \leq 2)$	0 1 2 3 4 5 6 7 8	$P(X < \quad)$
$P(2 < X < 7)$	0 1 2 3 4 5 6 7 8	$P(\quad \leq X \leq \quad)$
$P(X \geq 4)$	0 1 2 3 4 5 6 7 8	$P(X > \quad)$
$P(X < 3)$	0 1 2 3 4 5 6 7 8	$P(X \leq \quad)$
$P(X = 1)$	0 1 2 3 4 5 6 7 8	$P(\quad < X < \quad)$
$P(5 \leq X \leq 7)$	0 1 2 3 4 5 6 7 8	$P(\quad < X < \quad)$

PHOTOCOPYING OF THIS PAGE IS RESTRICTED UNDER LAW.
ISBN: 9780170389372

Words

Possible wording	The values that X can take are highlighted:	Notation
P(X **equals** 5) P(X is **the same as** 5) P(X is **exactly** 5)	0 1 2 3 4 **5** 6 7 8	$P(X = 5)$ $P(4 < X < 6)$
P(X is **more than** 5) P(X is **greater than** 5) P(X is **over** 5) P(X **exceeds** 5)	0 1 2 3 4 5 **6 7 8**	$P(X > 5)$ $P(X \geq 6)$
P(X is **less than** 5) P(X is **fewer than** 5) P(X **is under** 5)	**0 1 2 3 4** 5 6 7 8	$P(X < 5)$ $P(X \leq 4)$
P(X is **greater than or equal to** 5) P(X is **at least** 5) P(X is **no(t) less than** 5) P(X is 5 **or more**)	0 1 2 3 4 **5 6 7 8**	$P(X \geq 5)$ $P(X > 4)$
P(X is **less than or equal to** 5) P(X is 5 **or less**) P(X is **no(t) more than** 5) P(X is **at most** 5)	**0 1 2 3 4 5** 6 7 8	$P(X \leq 5)$ $P(X < 6)$
P(X is **between** 1 and 4)	0 1 **2 3** 4 5 6 7 8	$P(1 < X < 4)$ $P(2 \leq X \leq 3)$
P(X is **between** 1 and 4 **inclusive**)	0 **1 2 3 4** 5 6 7 8	$P(1 \leq X \leq 4)$ $P(0 < X < 5)$

Complete the table.

Words	Highlight the values that X can take:	Notation(s)
P(X is exactly 4)	0 1 2 3 4 5 6 7 8	
P(X is greater than 2)	0 1 2 3 4 5 6 7 8	
P(X is between 3 and 7)	0 1 2 3 4 5 6 7 8	
P(X is less than 5)	0 1 2 3 4 5 6 7 8	
P(X is at least 6)	0 1 2 3 4 5 6 7 8	

Words	Highlight the values that X can take:	Notation(s)
P(X is between 1 and 4 inclusive)	0 1 2 3 4 5 6 7 8	
P(X is 5 or less)	0 1 2 3 4 5 6 7 8	
P(X is greater than or equal to 1)	0 1 2 3 4 5 6 7 8	
P(X is under 7)	0 1 2 3 4 5 6 7 8	
P(X is over 6)	0 1 2 3 4 5 6 7 8	
P(X is 2 or more)	0 1 2 3 4 5 6 7 8	
P(X is more than 5)	0 1 2 3 4 5 6 7 8	
P(X is not more than 3)	0 1 2 3 4 5 6 7 8	
P(X exceeds 4)	0 1 2 3 4 5 6 7 8	
P(X is not less than 7)	0 1 2 3 4 5 6 7 8	
P(X is less than or equal to 5)	0 1 2 3 4 5 6 7 8	
P(X is at most 6)	0 1 2 3 4 5 6 7 8	

PHOTOCOPYING OF THIS PAGE IS RESTRICTED UNDER LAW.
ISBN: 9780170389372

Probability revision

Ways of expressing probabilities:

- Probabilities can be expressed as decimals, fractions or percentages.
- We usually use decimals because they are very easily compared.

Range of values that probability can take:

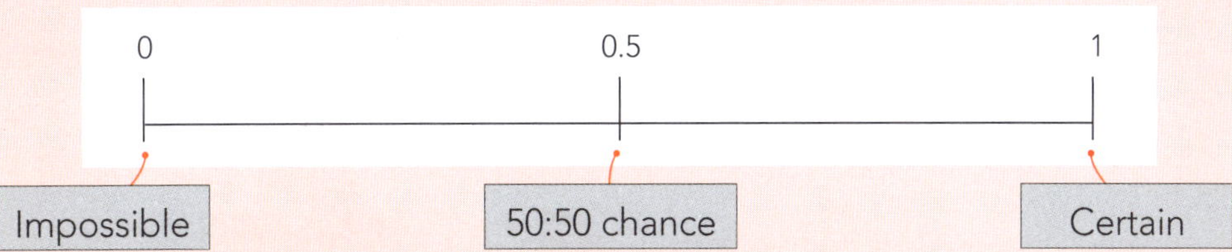

Impossible — 50:50 chance — Certain

Ways of calculating probabilities:

1 Equally likely outcomes: Probability $= \dfrac{\text{number of favourable outcomes}}{\text{total possible outcomes}}$

Example: For a 52-card pack, P(ace) $= \dfrac{4}{52}$

$= 0.0769$

2 Long run relative frequency: Probability $= \dfrac{\text{number of times an event occurs}}{\text{total number of trials}}$

Example:

P(Mike bikes to school) $= \dfrac{\text{number of times he has biked to school in the last year}}{\text{total number of school days in the last year}}$

$= \dfrac{94}{200}$

$= 0.47$

Combining probabilities:

and ⇒ **x**
or ⇒ **+**

Examples:

1 If you draw a card from a 52-card pack and then toss a die:
the probability of getting a heart **and** then a rolling a two $= \dfrac{13}{52} \times \dfrac{1}{6}$

$= \dfrac{13}{312}$

$= 0.041\dot{6}$

2 If you draw a card from a 52-card pack:
the probability of getting a two **or** a black seven $= \dfrac{4}{52} + \dfrac{2}{52}$

$= 0.1154$

ISBN: 9780170389372
PHOTOCOPYING OF THIS PAGE IS RESTRICTED UNDER LAW.

Expected number of outcomes: Probability = P(event) x number of trials

Example: If P(Eru bikes to school) = 0.68, and there are 50 days in the term, then:
Expected number of times Eru bikes to school in the term = 0.68 x 50 = 34

Frequency graphs:

Example: The graph below shows the number of Level 3 credits earned by 77 Year 13 students before the end of Term 1.

a What is the probability that a student earned exactly 15 Level 3 credits during the first term?

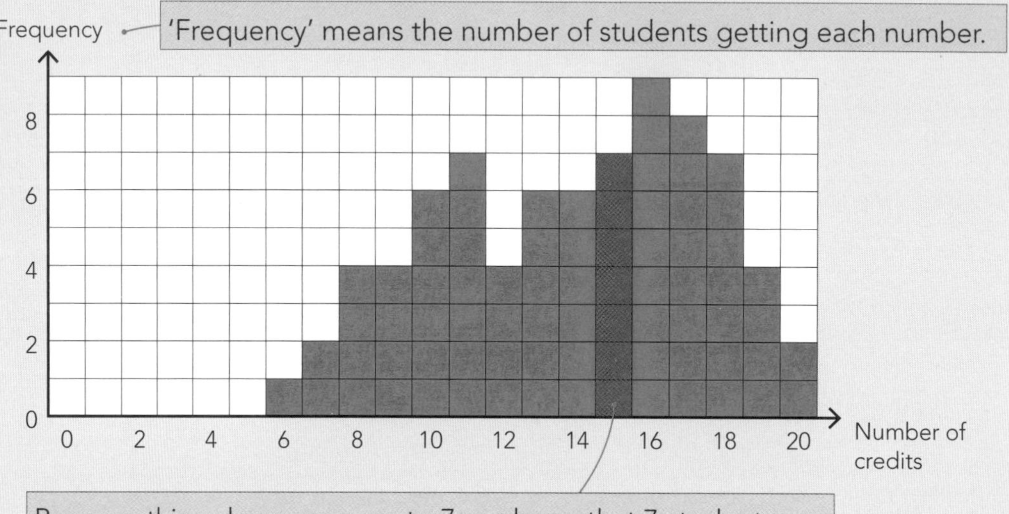

Because this column goes up to 7, we know that 7 students got 15 credits. P(15) = $\frac{7}{77} = 0.\dot{0}\dot{9}$

b What is the probability that a student earned fewer than 10 credits?

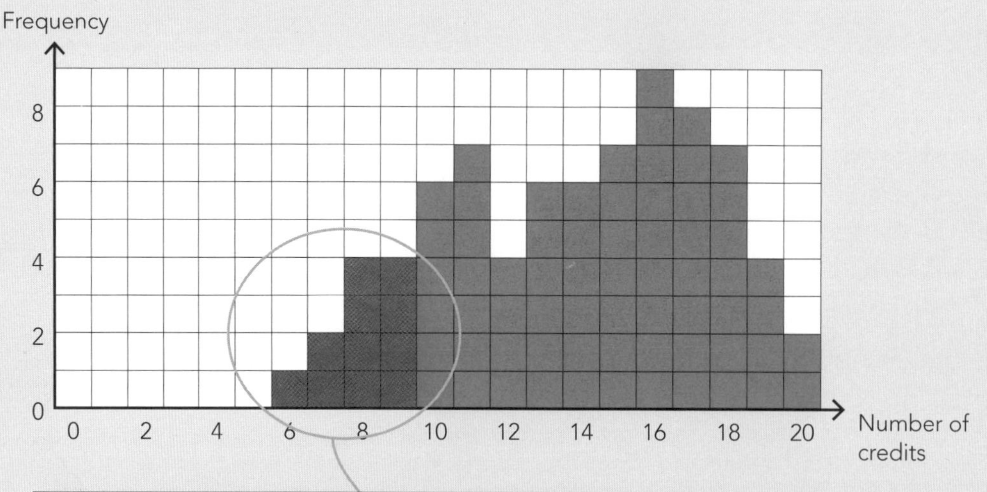

Because there are 11 students in the columns to the left of 10, and there were 77 students in total, the probability that a student earned fewer than 10 is $\frac{11}{77}$ = 0.1429.

PHOTOCOPYING OF THIS PAGE IS RESTRICTED UNDER LAW.
ISBN: 9780170389372

Answer the following questions.

1 Place the following probabilities in their correct order, from least likely to most likely.

0.1429 15% $\frac{2}{11}$ $\frac{1}{7}$ 0.181

____

2 A regular card pack has 52 cards. If you draw one card at random, write down the probability of:

a drawing a five ______________

b drawing a spade ______________

c drawing an ace or a two ______________

d drawing a picture card ______________

e not drawing a heart ______________

f drawing a 2, 4, 6, 8 or 10 ______________

3 During a school year of 200 days, Nikau biked to school 76 times, he walked 37 times, he skateboarded 63 times and his mother drove him 24 times. Write down the probability that:

a he skateboarded to school ______________

b he walked or biked to school ______________

c his mother didn't drive him to school ______________

d he neither skateboarded nor walked ______________

4 The probability that Kath walks to school is 0.45, and she has a Statistics class on four days out of five. Calculate the probability that on any particular day:

a she walks to school and she has a Statistics class

____

b she neither walks to school nor has a Statistics class

____

c she walks to school but does not have a Statistics class

____

5 In the past, the probability that a Year 13 student attends the formal has been 0.93. If there are 156 Year 13 students this year, how many can be expected to attend the formal this year?

____

6 At another school, the probability that a Year 13 student brings a partner from a different school is 0.256. If 32 Year 13 students bring partners from different schools, how many Year 13 students were there at the formal?

---

7 At Paradise High School one eighth of students come from outside the school zone. If there are 120 students from outside the zone, what is the roll of the school?

---

8 A survey of 80 students asked for the number of days in a week that each student participated in some type of sport. The results are shown below.

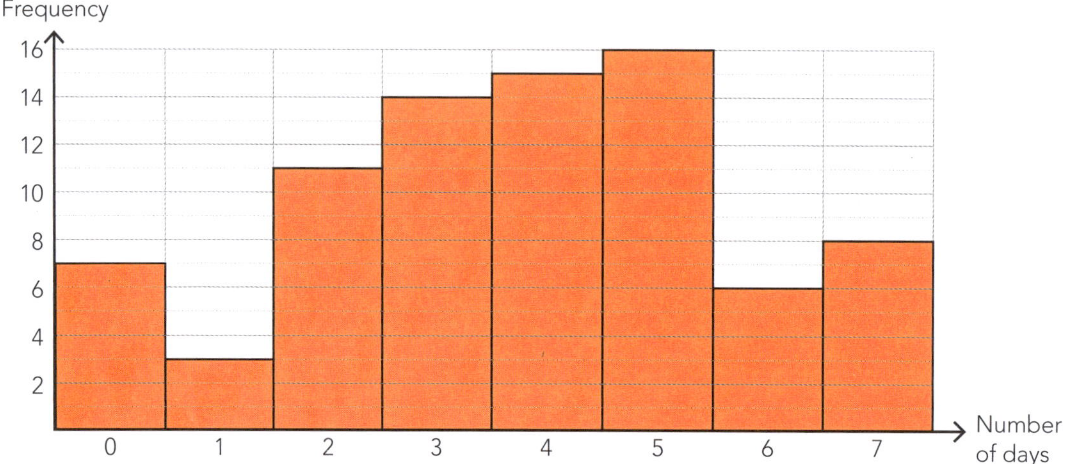

a Calculate the probability that a student participated in some type of sport every day of the week.

---

b Calculate the probability that a student participated in some type of sport on fewer than two days each week.

---

c Calculate the probability that a student participated in some type of sport on at least three but fewer than six days a week.

---

d Calculate the probability that a student participated in no sport at all, or participated in sport on at least six days per week.

---

e Two students are selected at random. What is the probability that both participate in some type of sport on fewer than two days per week?

PHOTOCOPYING OF THIS PAGE IS RESTRICTED UNDER LAW. ISBN: 9780170389372

True probability, experimental probability and theoretical (model) probability

True probability is almost always unknown. It is the **actual** probability that an event occurs.

Example: It is assumed that the probability of getting a head when a fair coin is tossed is 0.5. However, it is almost certainly not exactly 0.500000…. For instance, the extra weight of metal in the head, the way it is tossed, the surface on which it lands, etc. will affect the probability of getting a head.

Experimental probability is the probability obtained from an **experiment** or an **observational study**.

Example: If we toss a coin 50 times and get 22 heads, the experimental probability of a head is 0.44. The larger the number of trials, the closer the experimental probability will be to the true probability.

Theoretical (model) probability is the probability obtained from a **probability model**. Probability models are based on mathematical theory and observations about the behaviour of objects in an idealised world.

Example: The model estimate for the probability of a head when a fair coin is tossed is 0.5, on the assumption that both sides of the coin are equally likely to land on top.

You have probably already studied the normal distribution model. Other models that you may study this year are the following:

- Poisson distribution
- binomial distribution
- rectangular distribution
- triangular distribution.

Remember:

- Models must always be applied in context.
- There can be situations where no model fits.
- Sometimes more than one model may be appropriate.
- We can determine whether a particular model is a good fit for a situation by conducting an experiment or an observational study.
- Models will hardly ever fit a situation perfectly.

ISBN: 9780170389372 PHOTOCOPYING OF THIS PAGE IS RESTRICTED UNDER LAW.

Multiplication Principle

There are two ways to find out how many ways there are of arranging or selecting items:

1 Make a **list** of every possibility: this can be tedious or impractical.
or **2** Use the **Multiplication Principle** to calculate the number of ways.

Multiplication Principle:
If there are **p** different ways of filling position **1**
q different ways of filling position **2**
and **r** different ways of filling position **3**,

then there are **p** x **q** x **r** ways of filling the three positions.

Example 1: Jeremiah has 6 different shirts, 2 different ties and 4 pairs of trousers. In how many ways can he be dressed?

Shirts		Ties		Trousers	
6	x	2	x	4	= 48

Example 2: Ten people are running a race. In how many ways can the first three places be filled?

First		Second		Third	
10	x	9	x	8	= 720

Don't forget that the person who got first is no longer available to get second, etc.

Example 3: Calculate the number of possible different New Zealand car licence plates.

Letter		Letter		Letter		Numeral		Numeral		Numeral
26	x	26	x	26	x	10	x	10	x	10

= 17 576 000

Example 4: In how many ways can four people be arranged along a bench? The first person sits on the left, the second person sits next to the first, etc.

4	x	3	x	2	x	1	= 24

PHOTOCOPYING OF THIS PAGE IS RESTRICTED UNDER LAW.
ISBN: 9780170389372

Factorials

The last answer (4 x 3 x 2 x 1) is called a factorial and can be written as 4!

$$n! = n(n-1)(n-2)(n-3)(n-4)(n-5)\ldots 1$$

Examples: $5! = 5 \times 4 \times 3 \times 2 \times 1 = 120$

$2! = 2 \times 1 = 2$

$1! = 1$

$0! = 1$

Be careful! Think of this as the number of ways of seating 0 people on a bench.

Most calculators have a button for these because the values of factorials can be **very** large.

Example: In how many different ways can 12 people be seated on a bench?

$$12! = 479\ 001\ 600$$

Answer the following questions.

1 A menu contains three options for starters, four options for the main course, and two options for dessert. How many different ways are there of selecting a three-course meal?

____

2 There are six swimmers in a race. In how many ways can the first three places be filled?

____

3 An older system for car licence plates had letter, letter, numeral, numeral, numeral, numeral. How many different licence plates were possible under this system?

____

4 A security system for entering a bank's website requires a password, and then the correct selection of two different letters of the alphabet.

a How many different combinations of two alphabet letters are there if letters can be repeated?

____

b Calculate the probability of guessing the two correct letters if letters can be repeated.

____

c Calculate the probability of guessing two correct letters if repeats are not allowed.

____

ISBN: 9780170389372 PHOTOCOPYING OF THIS PAGE IS RESTRICTED UNDER LAW.

5 Corey has been given four different Easter eggs. If he finishes one egg before starting to eat the next one, in how many different orders can he eat his eggs?

____

6 PINs (Personal Identification Numbers) generally have four digits.

a How many PINs are there if any digit can occur in any position, and repeats are allowed?

____

b How many PINs are there if any digit can occur in any position but no digit can be repeated?

____

c How many PINs are there if digits can be repeated but the first digit cannot be a zero?

____

d Calculate the probability of correctly guessing a four-digit PIN if digits can be repeated but the first digit cannot be zero.

____

7 Nine members of a netball team have to be seated in a row for a photograph.

a In how many ways can they be arranged if any member can sit in any position?

____

b In how many ways can they be seated if the captain must sit in the middle seat?

____

c In how many ways can they be seated if the captain must sit in the middle seat and the two tallest players both must sit next to her?

____

8 In how many ways can five people be arranged in five seats in a car, if only three have full driver's licences?

____

9 Six girls and five boys are willing to play in a netball tournament. If the seven member team must have a minimum of three girls and three boys, how many ways are there of selecting the team?

____

____

PHOTOCOPYING OF THIS PAGE IS RESTRICTED UNDER LAW. ISBN: 9780170389372

Methods for displaying probability

Probability and frequency distribution tables and graphs

These display the probabilities or frequencies for a range of different events.

Example: The following are different ways of showing the results from 400 students who attempted the same achievement standard.

In a probability table:

Result	Not Achieved	Achieved	Merit	Excellence
Probability	0.24	0.47	0.23	0.06

Remember, these must add to 1.

In a probability graph:

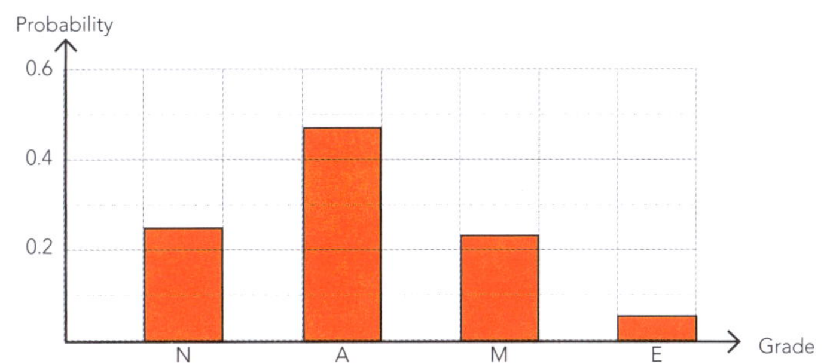

In a frequency table:

Result	Not Achieved	Achieved	Merit	Excellence
Probability	96	188	92	24

In a frequency graph:

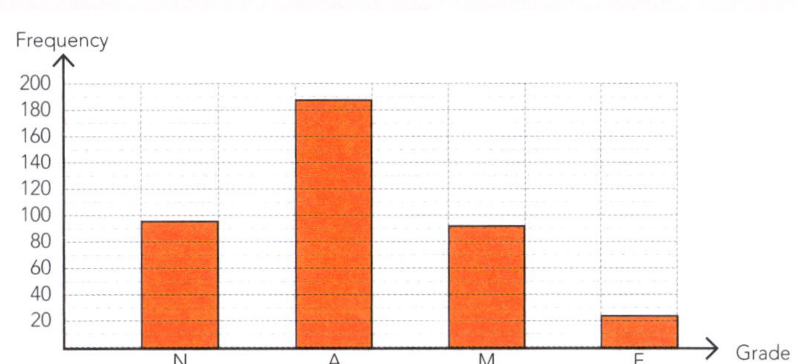

ISBN: 9780170389372 PHOTOCOPYING OF THIS PAGE IS RESTRICTED UNDER LAW.

Answer the following questions.

1 A group of Year 13 students was asked what form of driver's licence (if any) they had. The results are shown in the table.

No licence	Learner's licence	Restricted licence	Full licence
87	104	42	9

a Convert this frequency table into a probability table.

No licence	Learner's licence	Restricted licence	Full licence
0.3595			

b Draw a probability graph for this data.

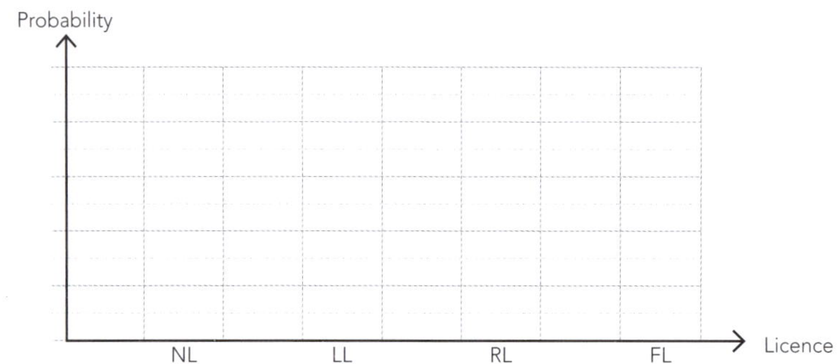

c Show two methods of calculating the probability that a Year 13 student at this school had some sort of licence. Explain fully why your two answers are different. Which would you consider more accurate?

d One term later, five more Year 13 students have earned their learner's licences, 11 who had learner's licences have passed their restricted licences, and four who had restricted licences have passed their full licences. Complete a new probability table for the Year 13 students. No Year 13 students have left and no new Year 13 students have joined the school.

No licence	Learner's licence	Restricted licence	Full licence

PHOTOCOPYING OF THIS PAGE IS RESTRICTED UNDER LAW.
ISBN: 9780170389372

2 At another school there are 381 Year 13 students. The table shows the probability distribution.

No licence	Learner's licence	Restricted licence	Full licence
0.3045	0.4672	0.1601	

a Complete the table.

b Complete the table below to show the numbers of students with each type of licence.

No licence	Learner's licence	Restricted licence	Full licence
116			

c Calculate the probability that a student had either a full licence or a restricted licence.

3 Hannah is playing a game of Snakes and Ladders and she is on square 96. These are the rules for the end of the game:

- When it is your turn, you throw a die and move forward the number of squares shown.
- If you land on the tail of the snake (e.g. square 97) you will slide down to square 65.
- To win you must land exactly on square 100. You may not overshoot.
- If you throw a number that will make you overshoot, you do not move during that turn.

The table shows the probability distribution for Hannah finishing the game in one, two or more than two turns.

a Show that the probability that she finishes the game in exactly two turns is $\frac{4}{36}$.

b Complete the probability table.

Turns to finish	1	2	> 2
Probability		$\frac{4}{36}$	

ISBN: 9780170389372 PHOTOCOPYING OF THIS PAGE IS RESTRICTED UNDER LAW.

4 An electronic game randomly selects two out of five different coins. They are a 10c, a 20c, a 50c, a \$1 and a \$2 coin.

a If the selection is made **without** replacement, complete the probability table for the total value of the two coins.

Total value	$T < \$1$	$\$1 \leq T < \$2$	$T \geq 2$
Probability			

b If the selection is made **with** replacement, complete the probability table for the total value of the two coins.

Total value	$T < \$1$	$\$1 \leq T < \$2$	$T \geq 2$
Probability			

c Harry is playing the game and wants to get at least \$1. Should he play the game with or without replacement? Why?

____

____

d Draw a graph of the probability distribution obtained for playing with replacement.

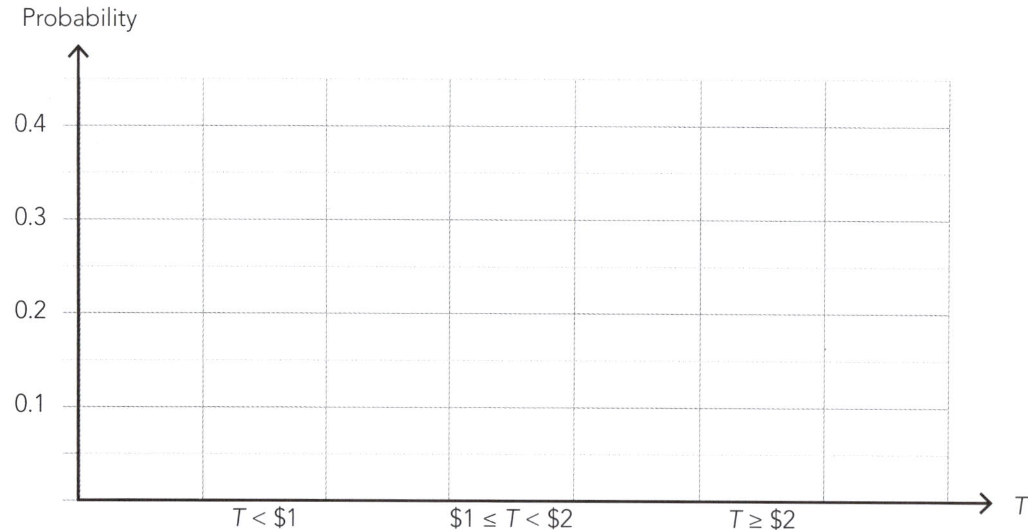

PHOTOCOPYING OF THIS PAGE IS RESTRICTED UNDER LAW.
ISBN: 9780170389372

Venn diagrams and probability tables

Venn diagrams	Symbols	Tables
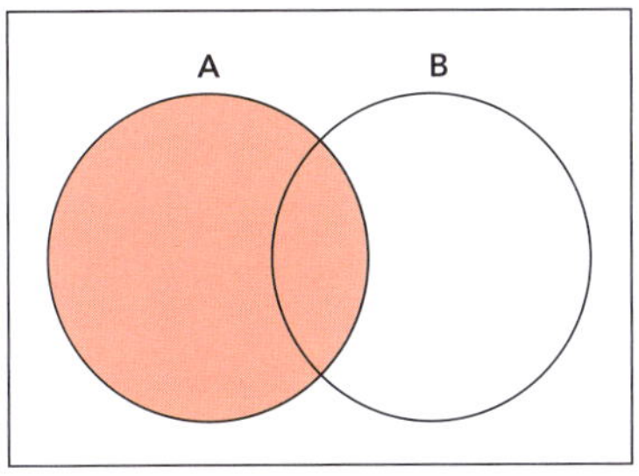	**P(A)** **'P(A)'** represents the probability of A occurring.	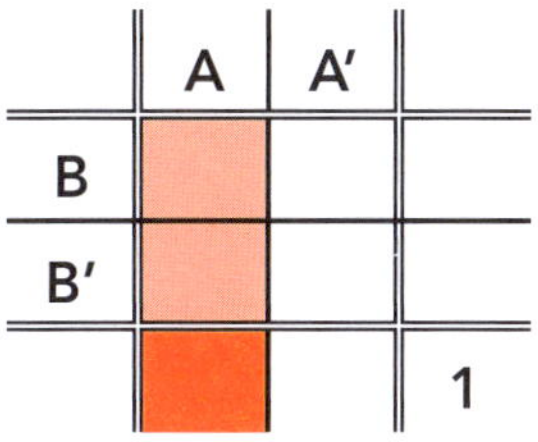
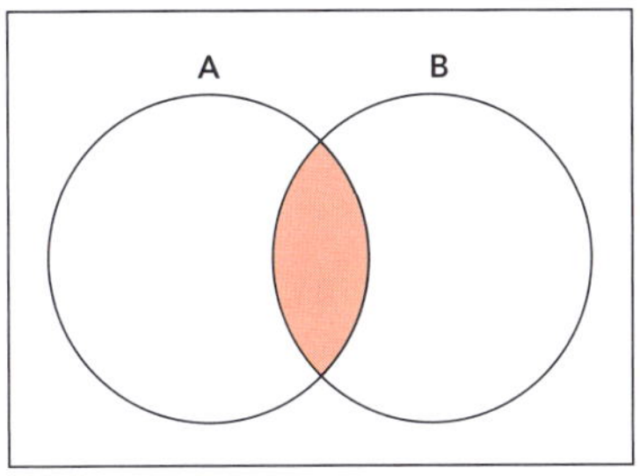	**P(A ∩ B)** **'P(A intersection B)'** represents the probability of both A and B occurring.	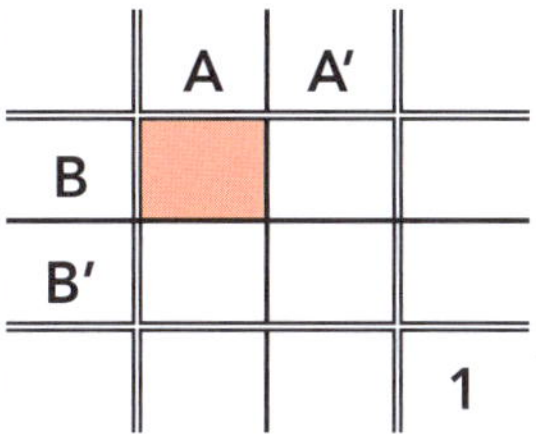
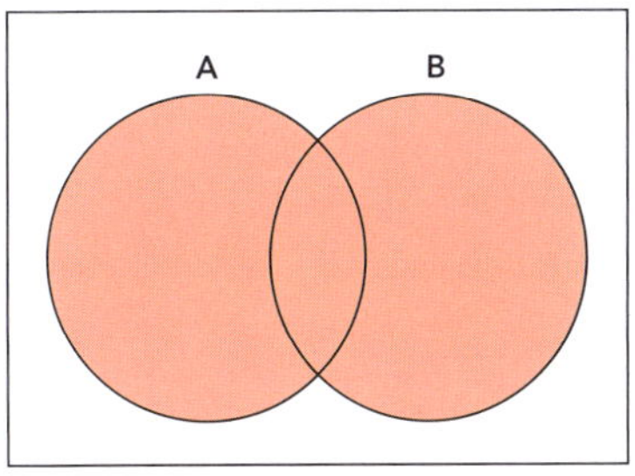	**P(A ∪ B)** **'P(A union B)'** represents the probability of A or B on their own or A and B together.	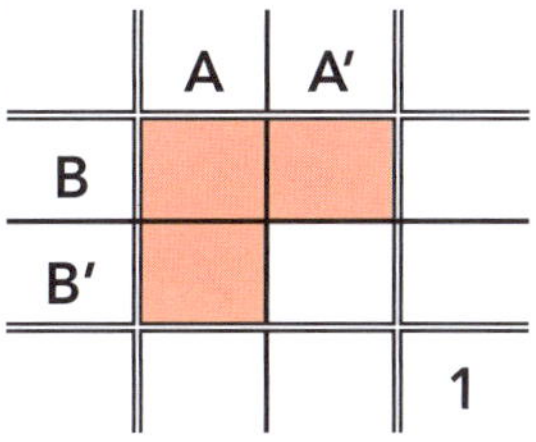
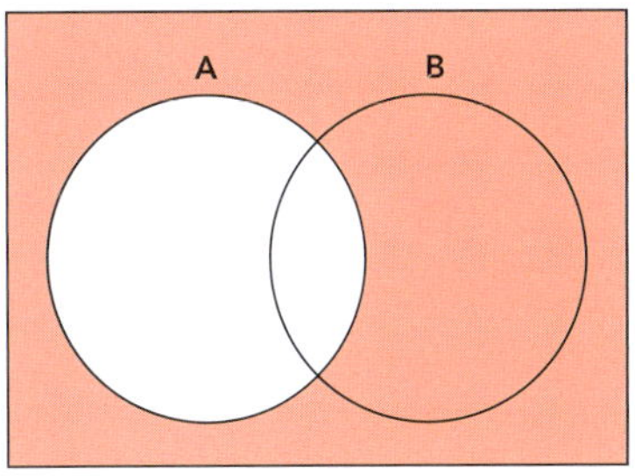	**P(A′)** **'P(A complement)'** represents the probability of 'not A' occurring	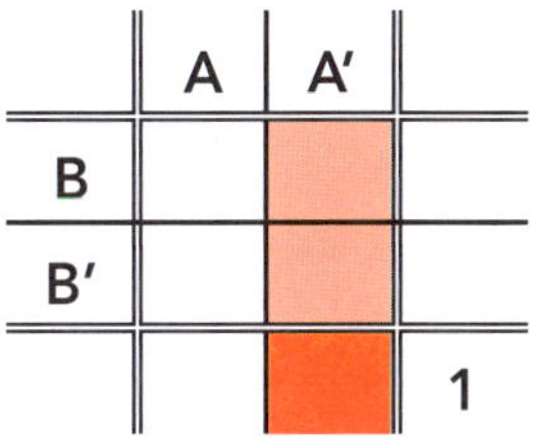
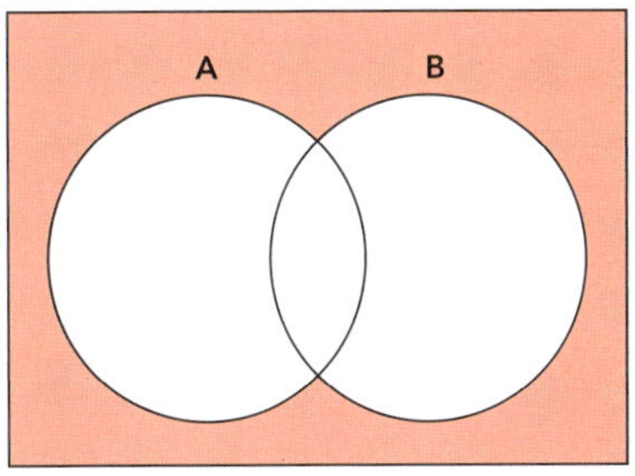	**P(A ∪ B)′ = P(A′ ∩ B′)** **'P(A union B complement)'** or **'P(A complement intersection B complement)'** represents the probability of neither A nor B occurring.	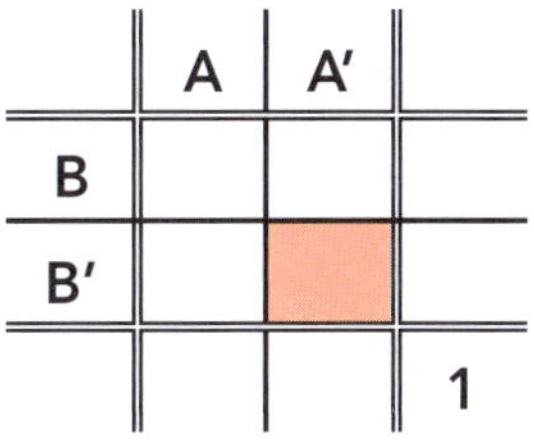

Probabilities with two overlapping groups

- The data may be given as frequencies, percentages, probabilities or fractions.
- Venn diagrams and tables are good ways of displaying the data.
- They are sometimes an alternative to probability trees.

Example 1: Draw a Venn diagram and a probability table to show the following probabilities: P(A) = 0.5, P(B) = 0.6 and P(A ∩ B) = 0.2. Use them to find P(A ∪ B).

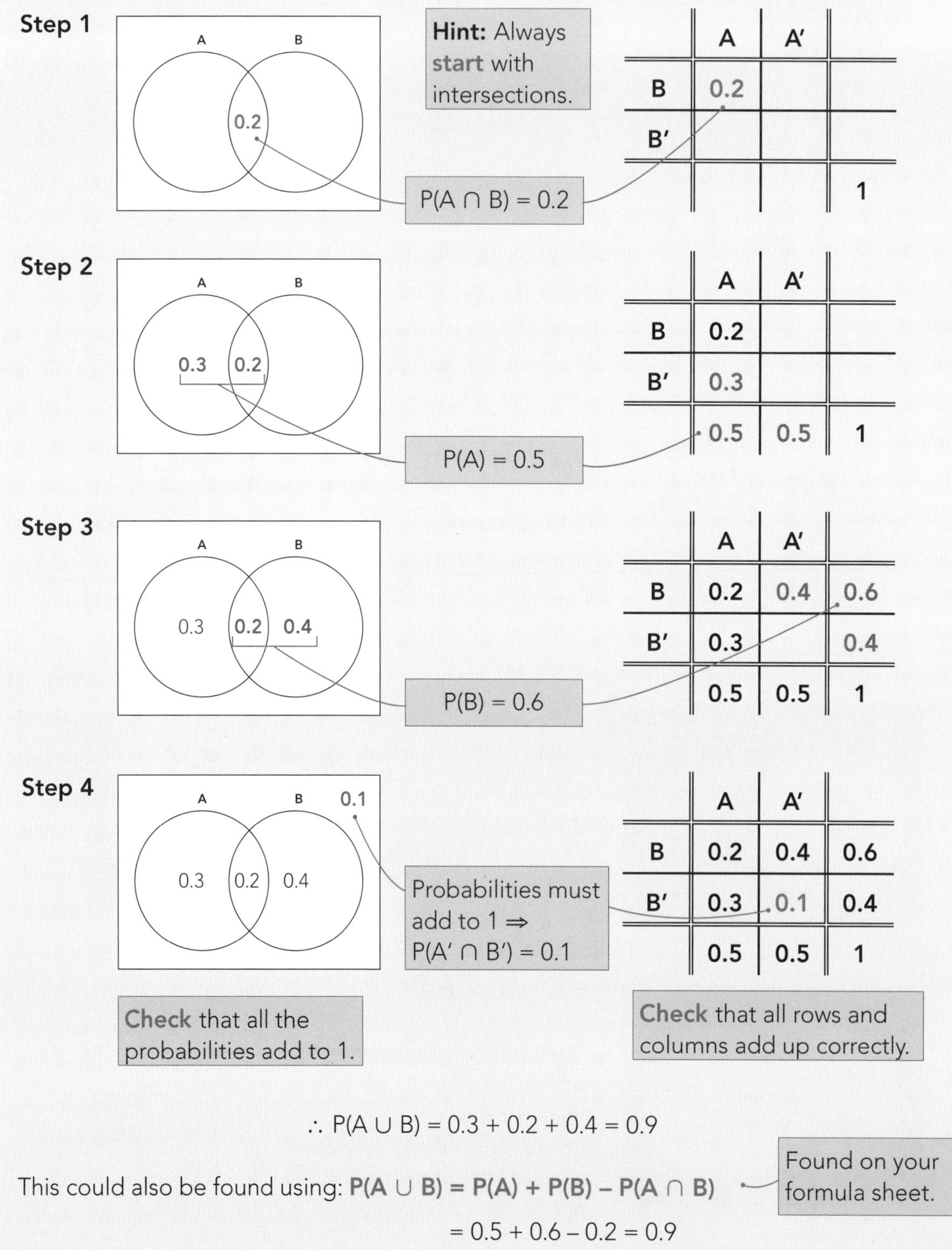

∴ P(A ∪ B) = 0.3 + 0.2 + 0.4 = 0.9

This could also be found using: **P(A ∪ B) = P(A) + P(B) − P(A ∩ B)** (Found on your formula sheet.)

= 0.5 + 0.6 − 0.2 = 0.9

PHOTOCOPYING OF THIS PAGE IS RESTRICTED UNDER LAW.
ISBN: 9780170389372

Example 2: For a group of 60 Year 13 students, 17 studied Calculus, 38 studied Statistics and 14 did neither. Draw a Venn diagram and a frequency table and answer the questions.

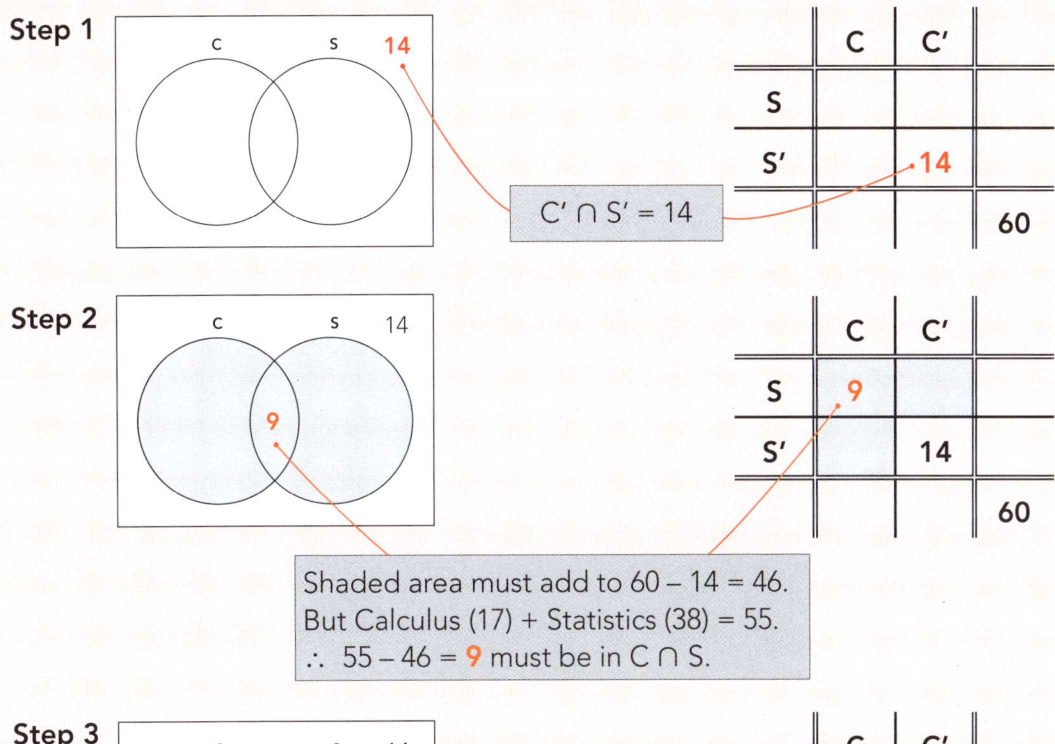

Step 3

C, S, 14: 8, 9, 29

	C	C′	
S	9	29	38
S′	8	14	22
	17	43	60

Use remaining information to help you complete the Venn diagram and table.

a Calculate the probability that a student studies Calculus but not Statistics.

$$P(C \cap S') = \frac{8}{60} = 0.1\dot{3}$$

b Calculate the probability that a student studies exactly one mathematical subject.

$$P(\text{one mathematical subject}) = \frac{8 + 29}{60} = 0.61\dot{6}$$

Notice that the table gives you far more information than the Venn diagram.

ISBN: 9780170389372 PHOTOCOPYING OF THIS PAGE IS RESTRICTED UNDER LAW.

Answer the following questions.

1 Complete the Venn diagram and the probability table to show the following:
P(A) = 0.4, P(A ∩ B) = 0.3 and P(B) = 0.5.

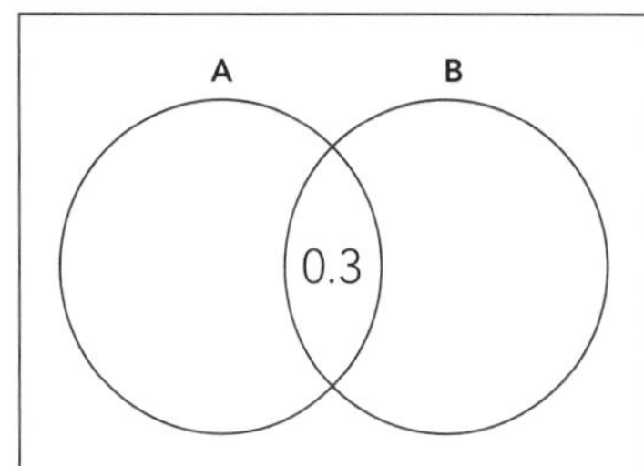

	A	A′
B	0.3	
B′		

Shade the areas to help you find the following probabilities.

a P(A ∪ B)

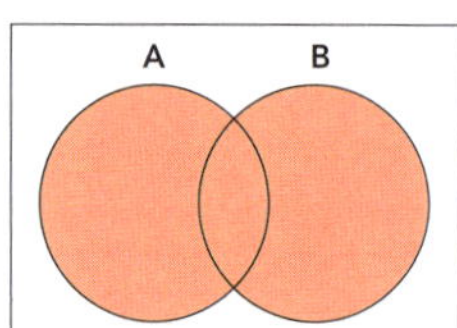

	A	A′
B		
B′		

0.6

b P(A′)

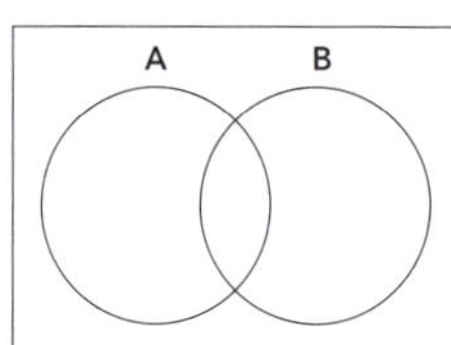

	A	A′
B		
B′		

____

c P(A ∩ B)

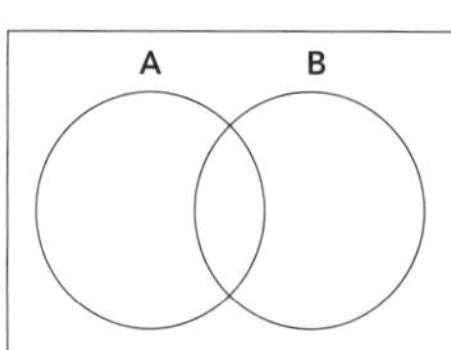

	A	A′
B		
B′		

____

d P(A ∩ B)′

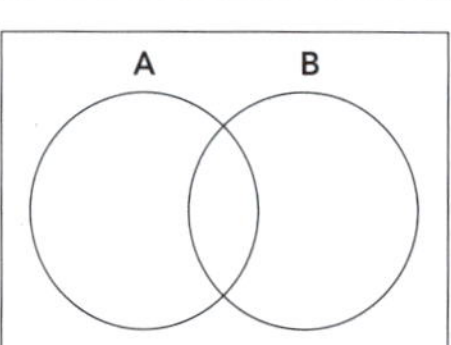

	A	A′
B		
B′		

____

e P(A′ ∩ B′)

	A	A′
B		
B′		

____

f P(A ∪ B)′

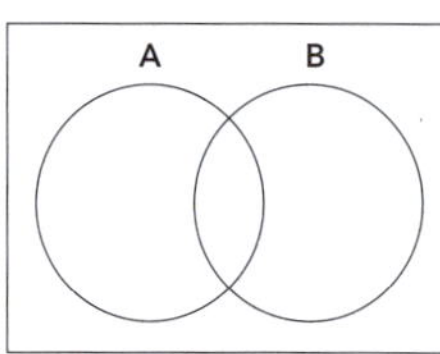

	A	A′
B		
B′		

____

g P(A ∩ B′)

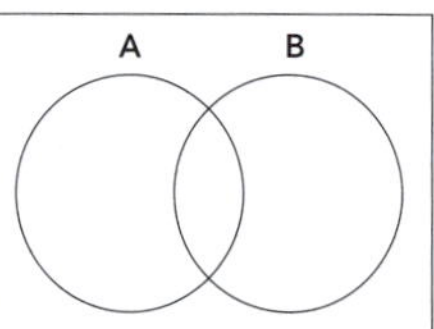

	A	A′
B		
B′		

____

 PHOTOCOPYING OF THIS PAGE IS RESTRICTED UNDER LAW. ISBN: 9780170389372

2 Complete the Venn diagram and the frequency table to show the following: for a group of 60 Year 13 students, 37 played a sport, 19 played a musical instrument and 9 did neither.

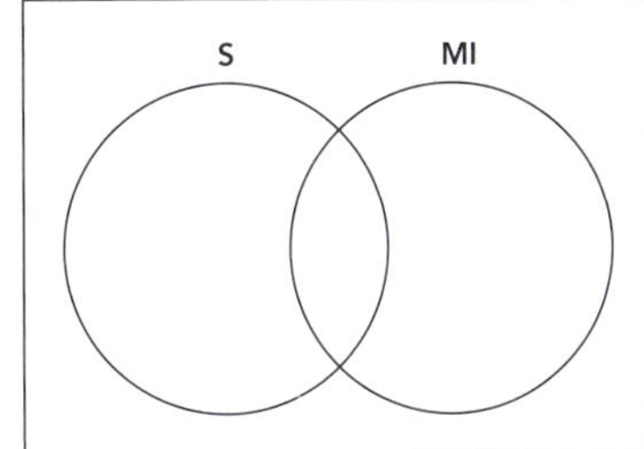

	S	S'	
MI			
MI'			

Shade the areas to help you find the following probabilities.

a P(S ∩ MI)

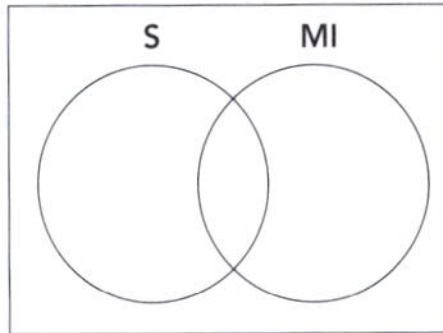

	S	S'	
MI			
MI'			

______

b P(MI')

	S	S'	
MI			
MI'			

______

c P(S ∩ MI')

	S	S'	
MI			
MI'			

______

d P(S ∪ MI')

	S	S'	
MI			
MI'			

______

e P(S' ∩ MI')

	S	S'	
MI			
MI'			

______

f P(S ∪ MI)'

	S	S'	
MI			
MI'			

______

g P(S' ∩ MI)

	S	S'	
MI			
MI'			

______

ISBN: 9780170389372 PHOTOCOPYING OF THIS PAGE IS RESTRICTED UNDER LAW.

3 A dairy owner records whether 80 of his customers buy milk or bread: 28 customers buy milk, 15 customers buy bread, and 25 customers buy milk but not bread. Complete the table and use it to calculate the probability that a customer buys bread but not milk.

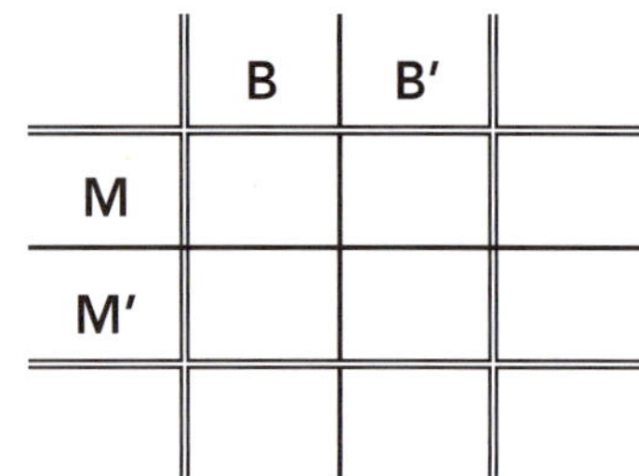

	B	B′	
M			
M′			

P = ______________________

4 An analysis of TV programmes watched on a particular night revealed that 62% watched *One News*, 7% watched both *The Bachelor* and *One News*, and 21% watched *The Bachelor* but not *One News*.

a Complete the table and use it to calculate the percentage of people who watched neither.

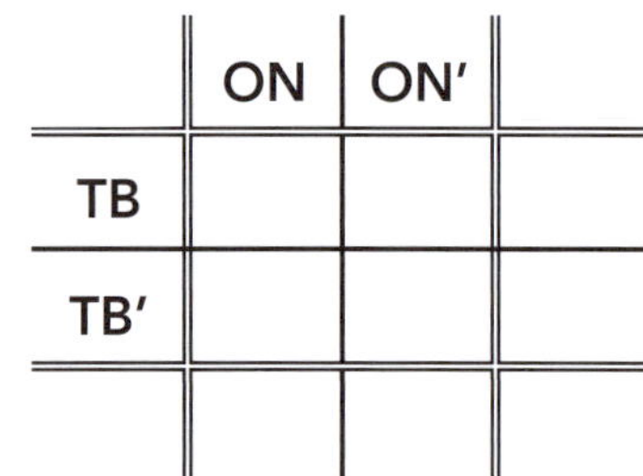

	ON	ON′	
TB			
TB′			

P = ______________________

b What proportion of those who watched *One News*, also watched *The Bachelor*?

____

c What proportion of those who didn't watch *One News*, watched *The Bachelor*?

____

5 In Year 13 at Paradise High School, 31% of students study Classics. The probability that a Year 13 student doesn't take History is 0.72, and 78% of Year 13 students take at most, one of these subjects.

a Calculate the probability that a student takes Classics but not History.

____

b What proportion of the students who took History, also took Classics?

____

c What proportion of the students who took Classics, also took History?

____

PHOTOCOPYING OF THIS PAGE IS RESTRICTED UNDER LAW.
ISBN: 9780170389372

6 An analysis was made of 120 people who used a track: 62 were female, of whom 16 cycled, while the rest walked; 36 were males who walked.

a How many people walked the track?

b Calculate the proportion of males who cycled. Calculate the proportion of females who cycled. Were males or females more likely to cycle, rather than walk, the track?

7 At Paradise High School, an end-of-term takeaway dinner is being organised for 150 Year 13 students. Students had to select their preferences from pizzas and hamburgers: 89 students were happy with pizzas, 78 were happy with hamburgers, and 23 didn't want either.

How many were happy with both pizzas and hamburgers?

Challenge: A third option was suggested: fish and chips.
Everybody was happy with at least one of the three options.

- 13 would be happy with both fish and chips and hamburgers, but not pizzas.
- 21 would be happy with any of the three options.
- 35 would be happy only with pizza.

How many people would be happy with both pizza and fish and chips?

ISBN: 9780170389372 PHOTOCOPYING OF THIS PAGE IS RESTRICTED UNDER LAW.

Probabilities with three overlapping groups

Once again, Venn diagrams and tables are good ways of displaying the data.

Example: A group of 215 Year 13 students were asked which of the subjects Art, Biology and Chemistry they were studying.

- 3 students studied all three subjects.
- 11 students studied Art and Biology.
- 26 students studied Biology and Chemistry.
- 5 students studied Chemistry and Art.
- 50 students studied Art.
- 80 students studied Biology.
- 60 students studied Chemistry.

Draw a Venn diagram to represent this situation and use it to calculate the number of students who take none of these subjects.

Step 1: Start with the overlapping groups.

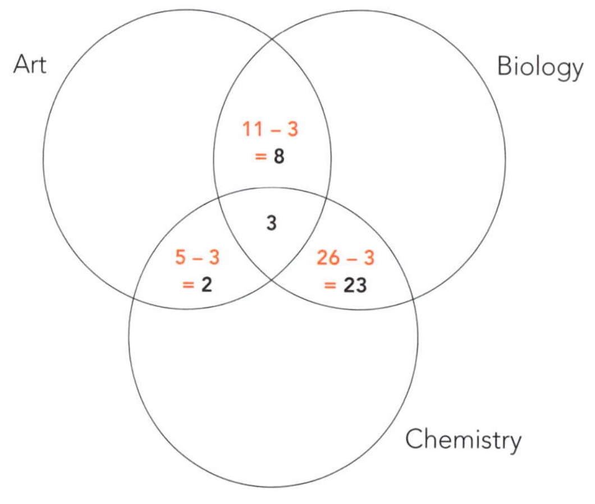

Step 2: Then complete the remaining groups.

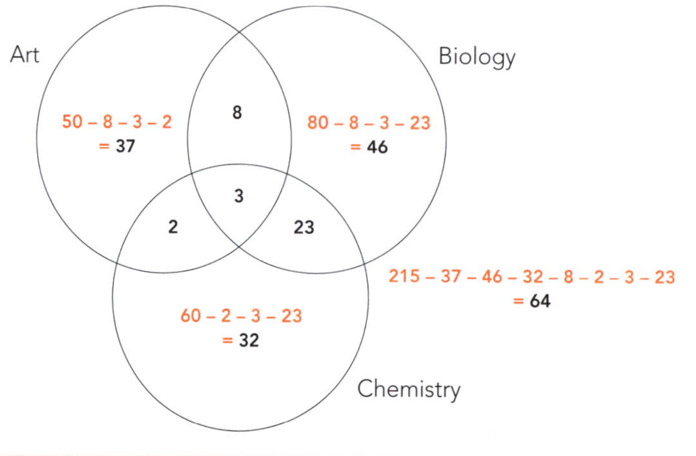

∴ Number who studied none of these subjects = 64

PHOTOCOPYING OF THIS PAGE IS RESTRICTED UNDER LAW. ISBN: 9780170389372

An alternative method: a modified frequency table.

Step 1: Start with the overlapping groups and the totals.

		Chemistry	Not Chemistry	TOTALS
Art	Biology	3	11 − 3 = 8	50
	Not Biology	5 − 3 = 2		
Not Art	Biology	26 − 3 = 23		215 − 50 = 165
	Not Biology			
TOTALS		60	215 − 60 = 155	215

Step 2: Complete the missing boxes in the order indicated.

		Chemistry	Not Chemistry	TOTALS
Art	Biology	3	8	50
	Not Biology	2	Step 1 50 − 3 − 2 − 8 = 37	
Not Art	Biology	23	Step 2 80 − 3 − 8 − 23 = 46	165
	Not Biology	Step 3 60 − 3 − 2 − 23 = 32	Step 4 155 − 8 − 37 − 46 = 64	
TOTALS		60	155	215

Remember that the total number studying Biology = 80.

∴ Number who studied none of these subjects = 64

Draw Venn diagrams or tables and answer the following.

1 A group of 215 Year 13 students were asked which of the subjects English, French and Geography they were studying.

- 9 students studied all three subjects.
- 22 students studied English and French.
- 11 students studied French and Geography.
- 36 studied Geography and English.
- 114 students studied English.
- 25 students studied French.
- 89 students studied Geography.

a Complete the Venn diagram to represent this situation.

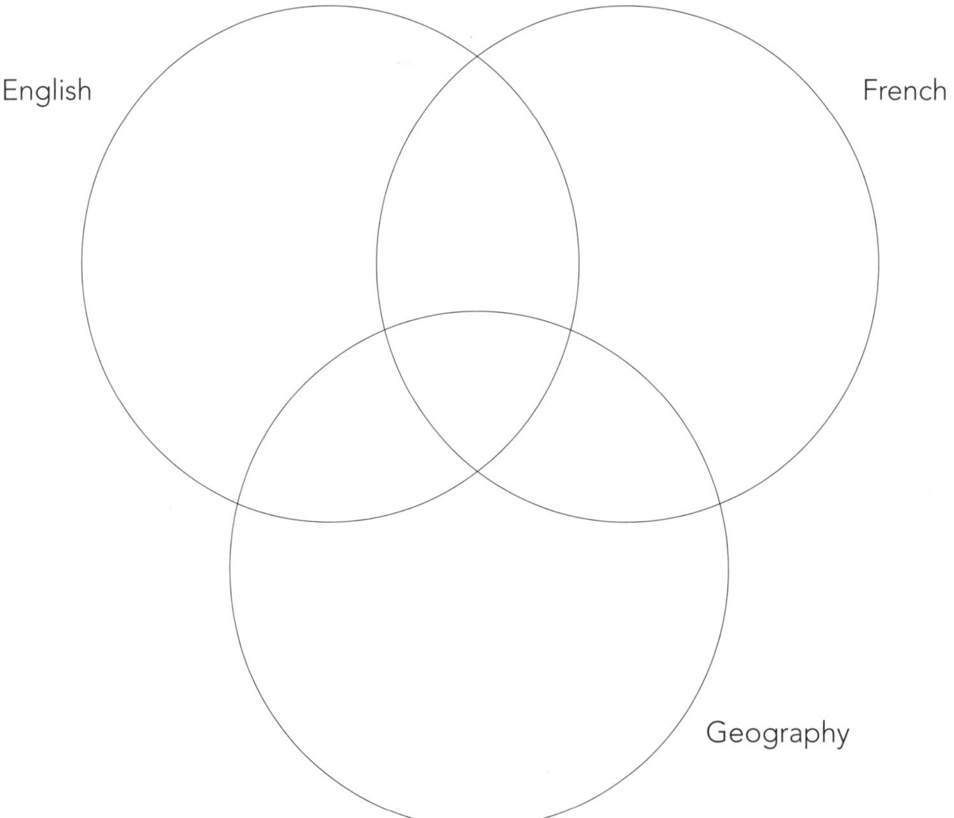

b Use it to calculate the number of students who study none of these subjects.

c Calculate the probability that a randomly selected student studies exactly two of these subjects.

PHOTOCOPYING OF THIS PAGE IS RESTRICTED UNDER LAW.
ISBN: 9780170389372

2 A survey of 100 students asked which of *Shortland Street*, *The Bachelor* and *One News* they had watched on TV the previous night.

- 22 students had watched *Shortland Street*.
- 42 students had watched *The Bachelor*.
- 4 students had watched *The Bachelor* and *One News*.
- 1 student had watched all three programmes.
- 7 students had watched *Shortland Street* only.
- 24 students had watched *The Bachelor* and neither *Shortland Street* nor *One News*.
- 46 students had watched none of the programmes.

a Complete the frequency table to represent this situation.

<table>
<tr><th colspan="2"></th><th>One News</th><th>Not One News</th><th>TOTALS</th></tr>
<tr><td rowspan="2">Shortland Street</td><td>The Bachelor</td><td></td><td></td><td rowspan="2"></td></tr>
<tr><td>Not The Bachelor</td><td></td><td></td></tr>
<tr><td rowspan="2">Not Shortland Street</td><td>The Bachelor</td><td></td><td></td><td rowspan="2"></td></tr>
<tr><td>Not The Bachelor</td><td></td><td></td></tr>
<tr><td colspan="2">TOTALS</td><td></td><td></td><td></td></tr>
</table>

b Use it to calculate the number of students who watched *The Bachelor* and *Shortland Street*.

____

____

c Calculate the probability that a randomly selected student watched *One News*.

____

____

3 Year 13 students were surveyed to find out the types of extracurricular school activities they were involved in. They were asked about involvement in sport, cultural activities and service to the school.

- 46% were involved in sport.
- 37% were involved in service.
- 29% were involved culture.
- 16% were involved in sport and service.
- 15% were involved in culture and sport.
- 12% were involved in all three types of activity.
- 26% of Year 13 students were involved in none of these activities.

a Draw a Venn diagram or frequency table to represent this situation.

b Use it to calculate the percentage of students who were involved in service or culture, but not sport.

____

____

c Of the students who were involved in sport, what percentage were also involved in culture?

____

____

PHOTOCOPYING OF THIS PAGE IS RESTRICTED UNDER LAW. ISBN: 9780170389372

4 Year 13 students were surveyed to find out where they got their lunches during a two-week period.

- 65% had brought lunches from home.
- 53% had bought lunches at the canteen.
- 71% used the canteen or brought lunches from home, but never bought at the local shops.
- 36% had lunch only from home.
- 7% had lunches from all three sources.
- 3% didn't eat any lunch.
- 2% had lunches from home and the local shops, but never from the canteen.

a Draw a Venn diagram or frequency table to represent this situation.

b Use it to calculate the percentage of students who bought from the local shops.

____

____

c Calculate the probability that a student who bought lunches from the local shops had also bought lunches from the canteen.

____

____

5 152 Year 10 students were surveyed to find out the school camp activities they enjoyed. The activities were the flying fox, the confidence course and the overnight camp.

- 96 enjoyed the flying fox.
- 95 enjoyed the overnight camp.
- 87 enjoyed the confidence course.
- 75 enjoyed both the flying fox and the overnight camp.
- 64 enjoyed both the overnight camp and the confidence course.
- 68 enjoyed both the confidence course and the flying fox.
- 5 enjoyed only the flying fox.
- 8 enjoyed only the overnight camp.
- 7 enjoyed only the confidence course.
- 29 didn't enjoy any of the activities.

a Draw a Venn diagram or frequency table to represent this situation.

b Use it to calculate the number of students who enjoyed all three activities.

____

____

c Calculate the probability that a student who enjoyed the flying fox also enjoyed the confidence course.

____

____

PHOTOCOPYING OF THIS PAGE IS RESTRICTED UNDER LAW. ISBN: 9780170389372

6 Year 13 students were surveyed regarding the options for an end-of-term meal: spaghetti bolognese, fried rice and a hangi. They had to state which of the three they would be happy with. The probabilities for each are listed in the table.

Meal	Probability
None of the meals	0.0292
Spaghetti bolognese only	0.175
Fried rice only	0.1208
Hangi only	0.4417
Spaghetti bolognese and fried rice	0.125
Spaghetti bolognese and a hangi	0.1375
Fried rice and a hangi, but not spaghetti bolognese	0.0458

a Draw a Venn diagram or frequency table to represent this situation.

b Use it to calculate the probability that a student would be happy with any of the three meals.

ISBN: 9780170389372
PHOTOCOPYING OF THIS PAGE IS RESTRICTED UNDER LAW.

Probabilities from tables of counts

Sometimes you have to calculate probabilities from more complex tables.

Example: Years 11, 12 and 13 students at Paradise High School were surveyed regarding driver's licences. The results are shown in the table.

Year	No licence	Learner's licence	Restricted licence	Full licence	Totals
11	86	26	0	0	**112**
12	36	47	18	2	**103**
13	18	20	31	25	**94**
Totals	**140**	**93**	**49**	**27**	**309**

a Calculate the probability that a surveyed student was in Year 12.

Probability = $\frac{103}{309} = 0.\dot{3}$

b Calculate the probability that a surveyed student was on a learner's licence.

Probability = $\frac{93}{309} = 0.3010$

c Calculate the probability that a surveyed student was in Year 12 **and** was on a learner's licence.

Probability = $\frac{47}{309} = 0.1521$

d Calculate the probability that a surveyed student was in Year 12 **or** was on a learner's licence.

Probability = $\frac{103 + 26 + 20}{309} = 0.4822$

Be careful not to count the 47 twice.

e Calculate the probability that a surveyed Year 12 student was on a learner's licence.

Probability = $\frac{47}{103} = 0.4563$

f Calculate the probability that a surveyed student who was on a learner's licence was in Year 11 or 12.

Probability = $\frac{26 + 47}{93} = 0.7849$

PHOTOCOPYING OF THIS PAGE IS RESTRICTED UNDER LAW.
ISBN: 9780170389372

Answer the following questions.

1 Years 11, 12 and 13 students at Paradise High School were surveyed regarding the number of school camps they had attended since starting secondary school. The results are shown in the table.

Year \ No. of camps	0	1	2	3	Totals
11	8	6	98	0	**112**
12	4	7	73	19	**103**
13	14	9	55	16	**94**
Totals	**26**	**22**	**226**	**35**	**309**

a Calculate the probability that a surveyed student had not been to any camp.

Probability = ______________________

b Calculate the probability that a surveyed student was in Year 13.

Probability = ______________________

c Calculate the probability that a surveyed student was in Year 11 **and** had been to two camps.

Probability = ______________________

d Calculate the probability that a surveyed student was in Year 11 **or** had been to two camps.

Probability = ______________________

e Calculate the probability that a surveyed Year 12 student had been to three camps.

Probability = ______________________

f Calculate the probability that a surveyed Year 13 student had been to at least one camp.

Probability = ______________________

g Calculate the probability that a surveyed Year 11 or 12 student had been to fewer than two camps.

Probability = ______________________

ISBN: 9780170389372 PHOTOCOPYING OF THIS PAGE IS RESTRICTED UNDER LAW.

2 A group of tourists were surveyed regarding the length of their stay and their main mode of transport while in New Zealand. The results are shown in the table.

	Tour bus	Hired vehicle	Public transport	Other	Totals
Less than two weeks	101	28	0	1	**130**
Between two and four weeks	128	154	3	2	**287**
Over four weeks	16	11	17	39	**83**
Totals	**245**	**193**	**20**	**42**	**500**

a Calculate the probability that a surveyed tourist stayed over four weeks.

Probability = ______

b Calculate the probability that a surveyed tourist travelled mainly by public transport.

Probability = ______

c Calculate the probability that a surveyed tourist stayed for over four weeks and travelled mainly by hired vehicle.

Probability = ______

d Calculate the probability that a surveyed tourist travelled mainly by tour bus or was in the country for between two and four weeks.

Probability = ______

e Calculate the probability that a surveyed tourist who travelled mainly by public transport, was in the country for more than four weeks.

Probability = ______

f Calculate the probability that a surveyed tourist who travelled mainly by hired vehicle, also stayed at least two weeks.

Probability = ______

g Calculate the probability that a surveyed tourist who stayed at least two weeks, also travelled mainly by hired vehicle.

Probability = ______

PHOTOCOPYING OF THIS PAGE IS RESTRICTED UNDER LAW.
ISBN: 9780170389372

3 A camping ground owner kept records of where guests came from, their age group and the type of accommodation they used. The results are shown in the table.

		Caravan or motor home	Cabin	Tent	Totals
New Zealander	Over 30	183	75	26	**284**
	Under 30	37	132	204	**373**
	Totals	**220**	**207**	**230**	**657**
Overseas	Over 30	149	27	6	**182**
	Under 30	19	64	166	**249**
	Totals	**168**	**91**	**172**	**431**
Grand totals		**388**	**298**	**402**	**1088**

a Calculate the probability that a guest was from overseas, and under 30 and stayed in a tent.

Probability = ______________________

b Calculate the probability that an overseas guest was under 30 and stayed in a tent.

Probability = ______________________

c Calculate the probability that a guest was under 30 and slept in a tent.

Probability = ______________________

d Calculate the probability that a guest was over 30 and didn't sleep in a tent.

Probability = ______________________

e Calculate the probability that a guest who slept in a cabin was under 30.

Probability = ______________________

f Calculate the probability that a guest who was under 30 slept in a cabin or a tent.

Probability = ______________________

g Calculate the probability that a guest who slept in a cabin or a tent was a New Zealander.

Probability = ______________________

ISBN: 9780170389372 PHOTOCOPYING OF THIS PAGE IS RESTRICTED UNDER LAW.

Probability trees

- These can be an alternative to probability tables and Venn diagrams.
- They are particularly useful when there is a **sequence** of events.

Example: In a particular region, 15% of the population is vaccinated against the flu. The probability that a vaccinated person catches the flu is 0.09, but 36% of unvaccinated people will catch the flu.

a Calculate the probability that a person is vaccinated and catches the flu.
b Calculate the overall percentage of people who will catch the flu.
c What percentage of those who catch the flu had been vaccinated?
d What percentage of vaccinated people caught the flu?

Steps:

1 Decide what the **events** are, and their order.
Event 1 will be that a person is vaccinated against the flu.
Event 2 will be that a person catches the flu.
Write the **events** at the **ends** of the branches.

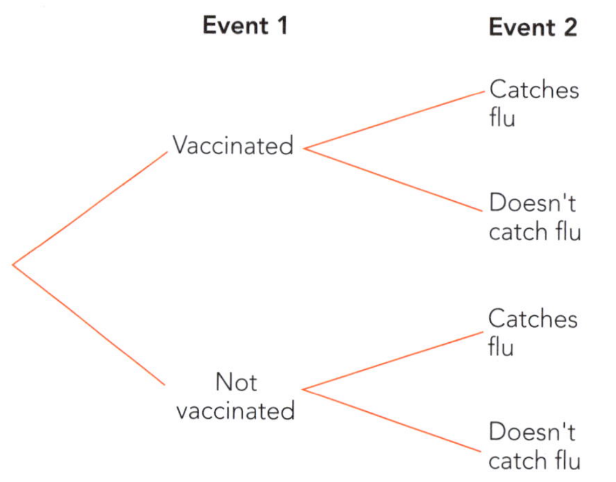

2 Add the **probabilities** of each event to the **middle** of each branch.

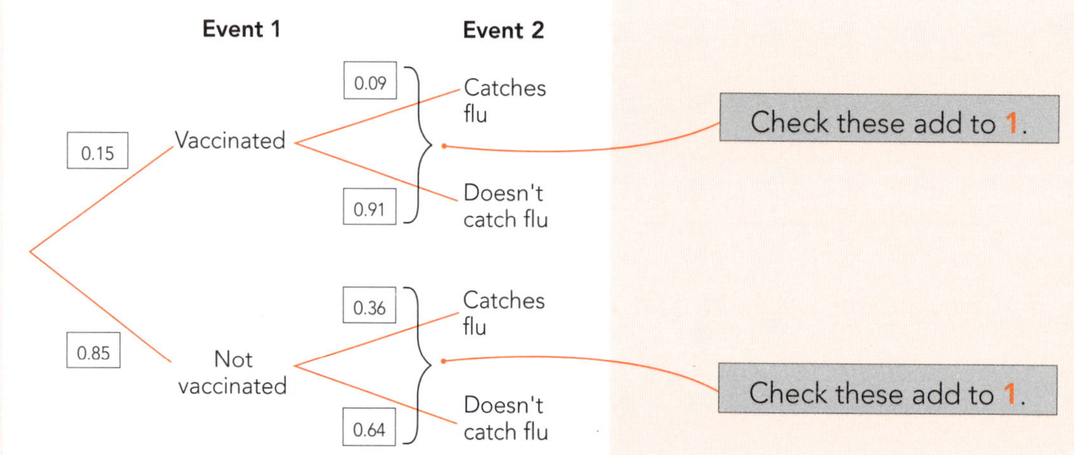

Check these add to 1.

Check these add to 1.

3 **Check** that the probabilities for every branch add to **1**.

PHOTOCOPYING OF THIS PAGE IS RESTRICTED UNDER LAW. ISBN: 9780170389372

4 **List** the outcomes at the ends of each branch, and calculate the probabilities at each end. You **multiply** the probabilities **along** each branch because Event 1 **and** Event 2 must occur.

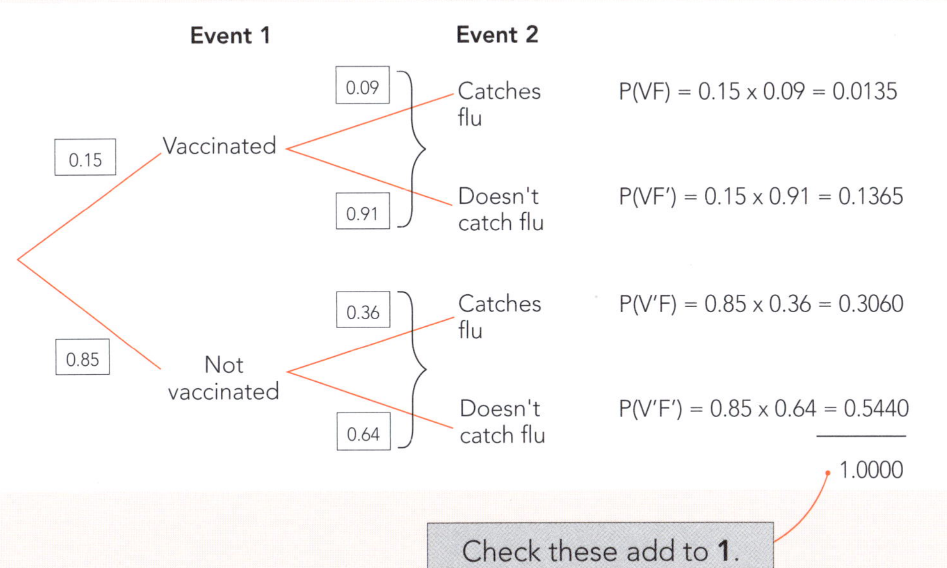

5 **Check** that your probabilities in the far right-hand column **add** to **1**. The reason is that one of VF **or** VF' **or** V'F **or** V'F' **must** occur.

6 In the columns on the right, highlight the event required, along with their probabilities. **Add** these to find the overall probability required.

Answers:

a P(a person is vaccinated and catches the flu) = 0.0135.

b Overall percentage of people who will catch the flu = 1.35% + 30.60% = 31.95%.

c Of those who caught the flu, what percentage had been vaccinated?

$$= \frac{\text{\% vaccinated people who caught the flu}}{\text{total \% catching the flu}}$$

$$= \frac{1.35\%}{1.35\% + 30.6\%}$$

= 4.23%

Percentage who are vaccinated **and** catch the flu.

Total percentage who catch the flu.

d Percentage of vaccinated people who caught the flu

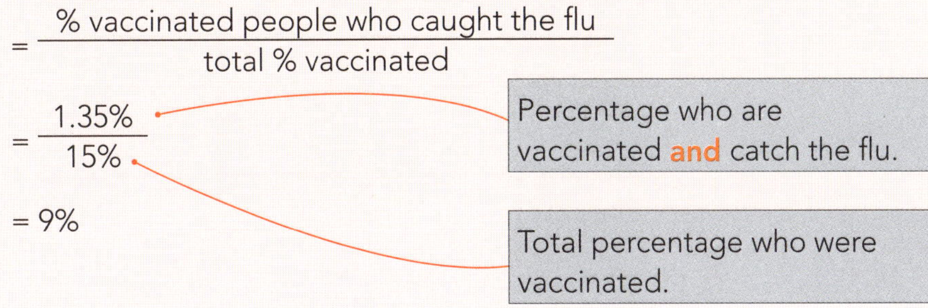

$$= \frac{\text{\% vaccinated people who caught the flu}}{\text{total \% vaccinated}}$$

$$= \frac{1.35\%}{15\%}$$

= 9%

Try these questions.

1 Of the Year 13 Paradise High School students, 52% are girls. The probability that a boy studies Statistics is 0.74, whereas the probability that a girl studies Statistics is 0.42.

a Complete the probability tree.

b Calculate the probability that a Year 13 Paradise High School student is a girl who doesn't study Statistics.

c Calculate the probability that a Year 13 Paradise High School student does not study Statistics.

d What percentage of Year 13 Paradise High School students are girls or study Statistics?

e What percentage of Year 13 Paradise High School students who study Statistics are girls?

f Convert this information into a probability table.

	S	S′	
G			
B			

PHOTOCOPYING OF THIS PAGE IS RESTRICTED UNDER LAW. ISBN: 9780170389372

2 Of 240 Year 13 students, 15% take Art. Of the students who take Art, 20 also take Design. There is a total of 54 Year 13 students who take design.

a Calculate the probability that a student takes both Art and Design.

____

b Use this to calculate the probability that a student who takes Art also takes Design.

____

c Complete the probability tree.

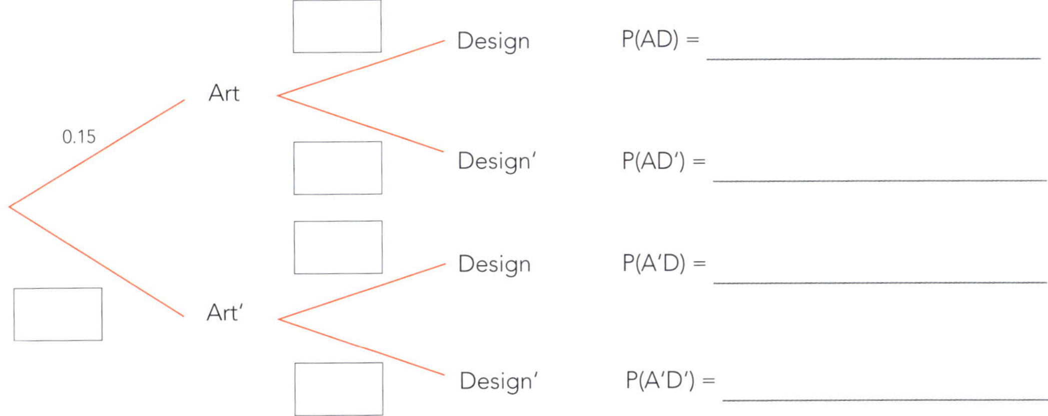

d Convert this information into a probability table.

	D	**D'**	
A			
A'			

e Calculate the probability that a student takes exactly one of these subjects.

____

f Calculate the probability that a student who doesn't take Art, takes Design.

____

g Calculate the probability that a student who doesn't take Design, takes Art.

____

h If two students are selected at random, what is the probability that both students take neither of these subjects?

____

ISBN: 9780170389372 PHOTOCOPYING OF THIS PAGE IS RESTRICTED UNDER LAW.

3 Amy and Ben have the opportunity to go on a luge. The probability that Amy does it is 0.7. The probability that both go on it is 0.63 and the probability that neither does it is 0.045.

a Draw a probability tree to illustrate this.

b What is the probability that just one of them goes on the luge?

c If Ben goes on it, what is the probability that Amy does it too?

4 Amy and Ben also have the opportunity to do a sky dive. The probability that Amy does it is 0.9. If Amy does it then the probability that Ben does it too is 0.4. The probability that exactly one of them does the sky dive is 0.56.

a Draw a probability tree to illustrate this.

b What is the probability that Ben does the sky dive?

c If Ben doesn't do it, what is the probability that Amy does the sky dive?

d Describe in words the relative likelihoods that Amy and Ben do the sky dive.

PHOTOCOPYING OF THIS PAGE IS RESTRICTED UNDER LAW.
ISBN: 9780170389372

5 An adventure company keeps records of which activities their clients do, and whether they are New Zealanders or they come from overseas. The table shows the results for jet-boating.

	Went jet-boating	Didn't go jet-boating
New Zealand	0.084	0.226
Overseas	0.561	0.129

a Use this data to complete the probability tree.

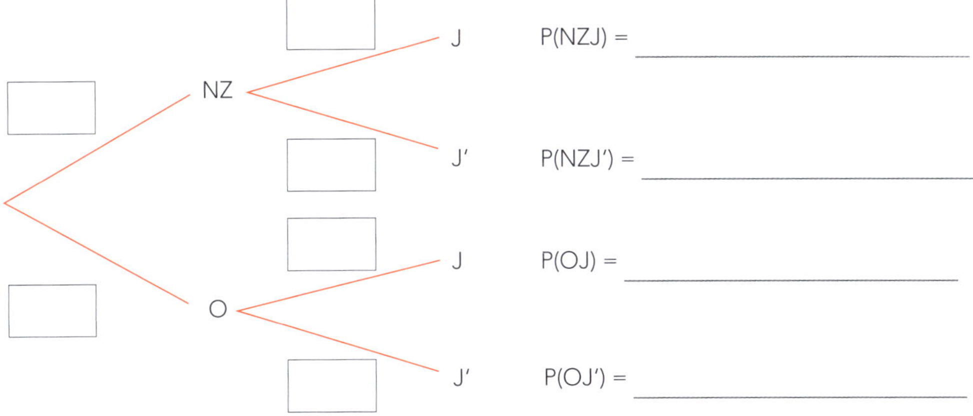

b What is the probability that a client was a New Zealander and went jet-boating?

c What is the probability that a New Zealander went jet-boating?

d What is the probability that a client who went jet-boating was from overseas?

e What is the probability that a client who was from overseas went jet-boating?

f If two clients are chosen at random, calculate the probability that both were clients from overseas who went jet-boating.

g Summarise for the company what this data tells you.

6 A regional health board keeps records of the numbers of babies who get the flu when they are under six months old. It also records whether the mother had a flu vaccination during the six months before the baby was born.

	Baby caught flu	Baby didn't catch flu
Mother vaccinated	0.0027	0.3511
Mother not vaccinated	0.0863	0.5599

a Use this data to complete the probability tree.

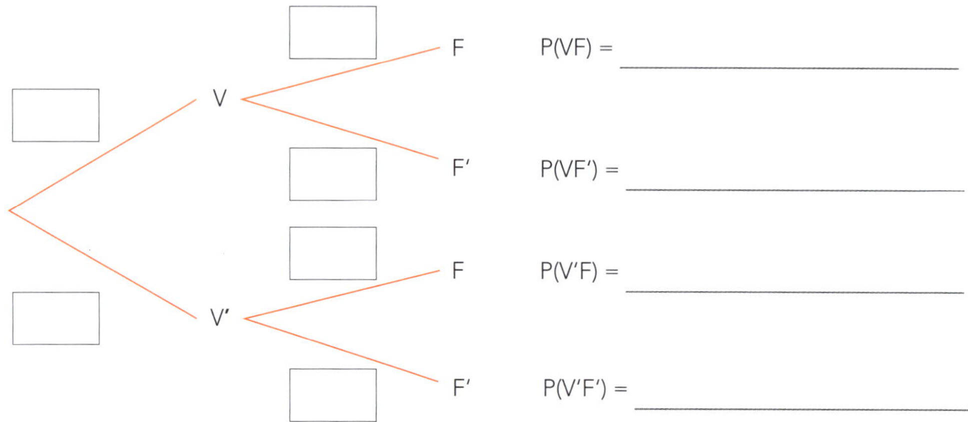

b What proportion of babies caught the flu?

c What is the probability that a baby who caught the flu had an unvaccinated mother?

d What is the probability that the baby of an unvaccinated mother caught the flu?

e What is the probability that a baby of a vaccinated mother caught the flu?

f If two mothers are chosen at random, what is the probability that one mother was vaccinated and had a baby that didn't catch the flu, and the other was unvaccinated and had a baby that caught the flu?

g Summarise the data for the health board.

PHOTOCOPYING OF THIS PAGE IS RESTRICTED UNDER LAW.
ISBN: 9780170389372

7 If the school badminton team wins its final game for the season, it will be the top team in its grade.

- The team's final game may be in week 9, or the team may have a bye in week 9, and then play the final game in week 10.
- For any game in week 9, the probability of a 'home' game is 0.5, and the probability of an 'away' game is 0.3. Otherwise the team will have a bye.
- If the team had a bye in week 9, it must have a game in week 10, and the probability that it will be a 'home' game is 0.65.
- The probability of winning a 'home' game is 0.7, and the probability of winning an 'away' game is 0.6. There is no possibility of a draw.

a Complete the probability tree.

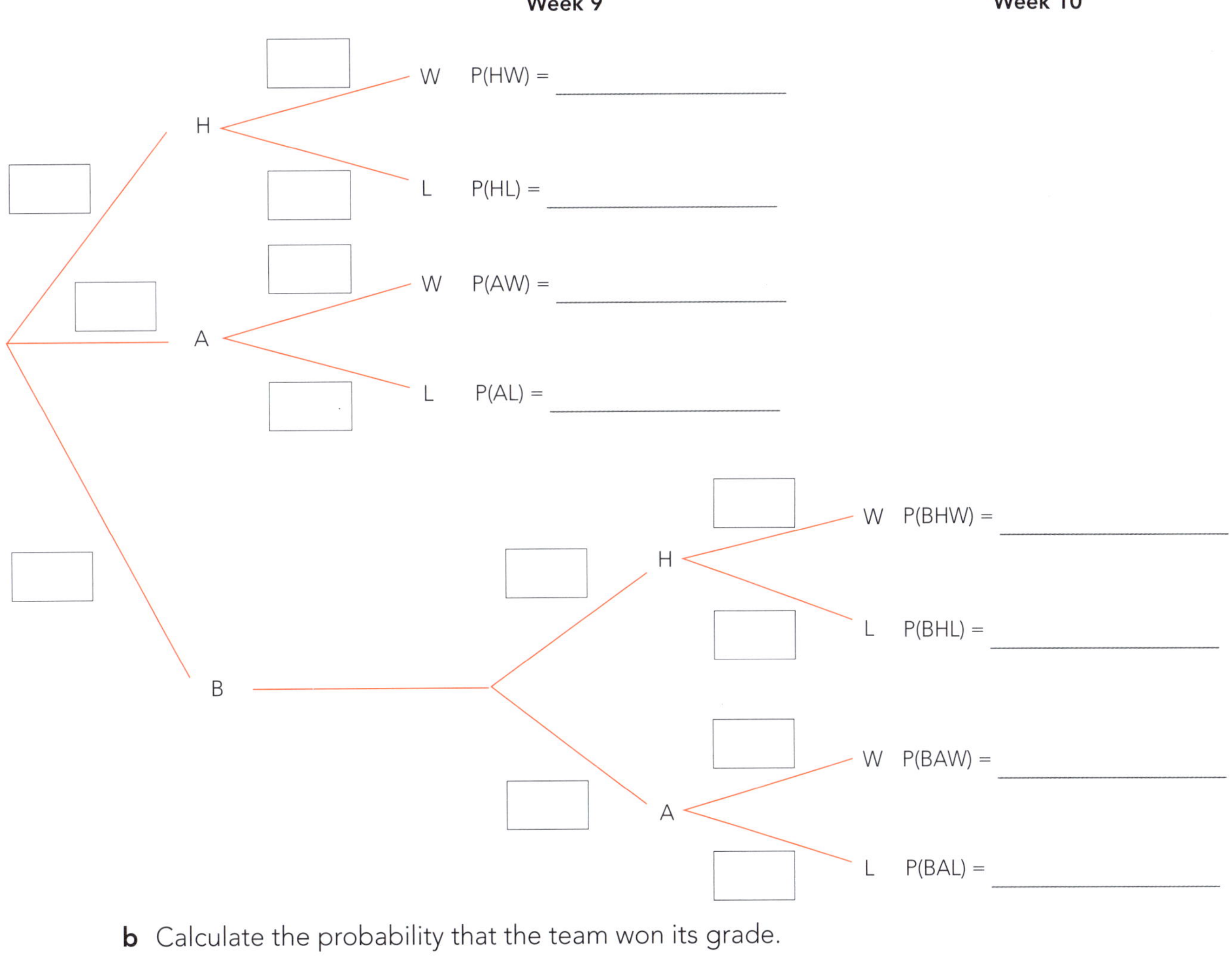

b Calculate the probability that the team won its grade.

____

c If the team won its grade, what is the probability that it won it in week 9?

____

d If the team had a bye in week 9, what is the probability that it won the grade?

____

ISBN: 9780170389372

8 There is an epidemic of goofy gorilla disease at the Primate Zoo, and some visitors catch it while they are there. There is a test for this, but it is not 100% reliable.

- Of those who catch the disease, only 80% will show symptoms.
- 95% of those who catch it and show symptoms will test positive for the disease.
- Of those who have the disease but don't show symptoms, 90% will test positive for the disease.
- Of those who don't have the disease, 8% will test positive.
- 24% of visitors to the park catch the disease.

a Draw a probability tree to illustrate this situation.

b Calculate the probability that a visitor to the Primate Zoo tests positive for the disease.

c What percentage of people who tested positive for the disease, actually had the disease?

d What percentage of people who tested negative for the disease, actually had the disease?

e Two visitors are selected at random. Calculate the probability that one caught the disease, showed symptoms and tested positive, while the other didn't catch the disease and tested negative.

 PHOTOCOPYING OF THIS PAGE IS RESTRICTED UNDER LAW. ISBN: 9780170389372

Interrelationships between events

Mutually exclusive (disjoint) events

- Mutually exclusive events **cannot both** occur at the same time.
- In a Venn diagram the circles **don't overlap**.

The probability of A **or** B: **P(A ∪ B) = P(A) + P(B)**
The probability of A **and** B: **P(A ∩ B) = 0**

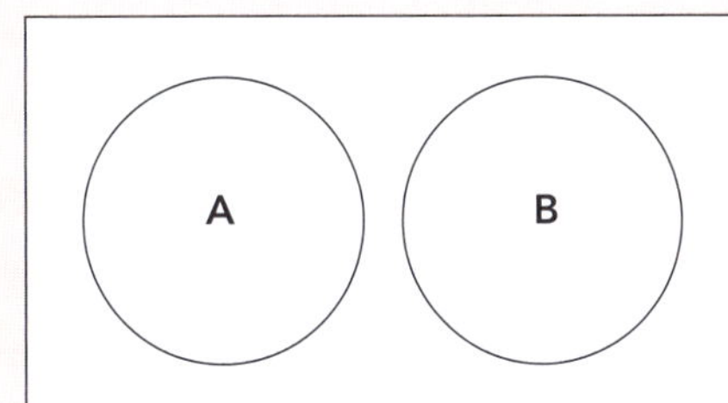

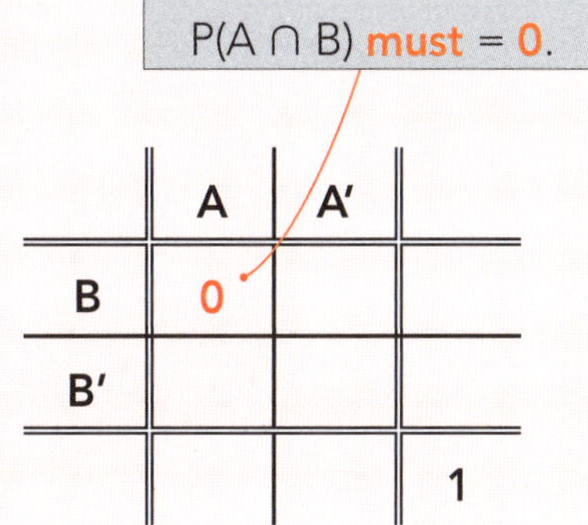

P(A ∩ B) **must** = 0.

	A	A′	
B	0		
B′			
			1

Example: In a normal 52-card pack, hearts and black cards are mutually exclusive. Find the probability of picking a heart or a black card.

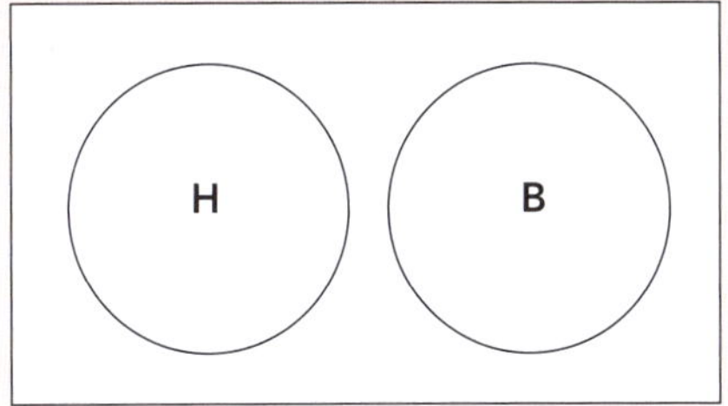

P(H) + P(B) = ¼ + ½
= 0.75

	B	B′	
H	0	0.25	0.25
H′	0.5	0.25	0.75
	0.5	0.5	1

In general: **P(A ∪ B) = P(A) + P(B)**
and
P(A ∩ B) = 0

ISBN: 9780170389372 PHOTOCOPYING OF THIS PAGE IS RESTRICTED UNDER LAW.

Events that are not mutually exclusive

Events that are not mutually exclusive **can both** occur at the same time.
In a Venn diagram the circles **overlap**.

The probability of A or B: $P(A \cup B) = P(A) + P(B) - P(A \cap B)$
The probability of A and B: $P(A \cap B) \neq 0$

You need to subtract this because otherwise you would be counting the overlapping part twice.

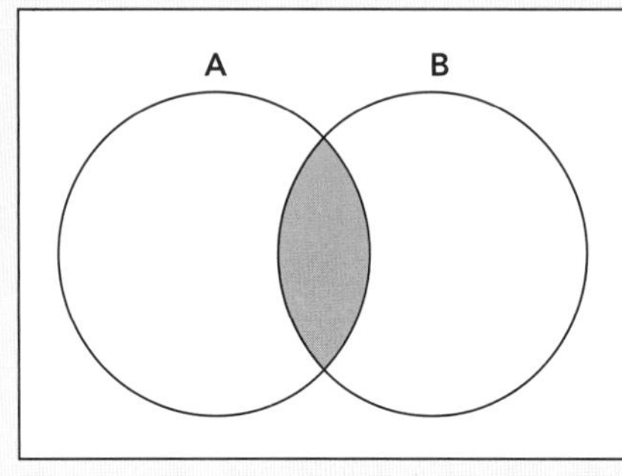

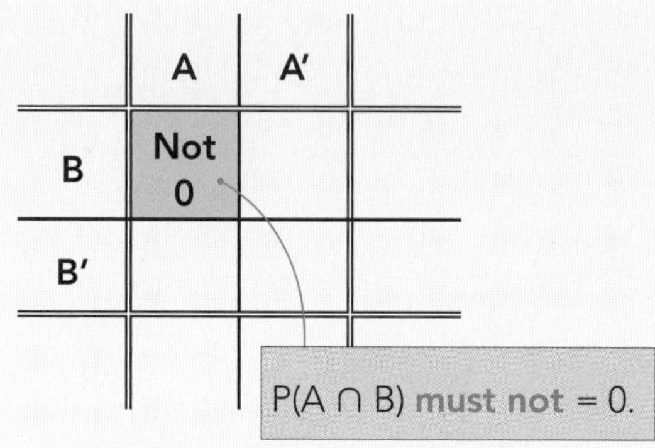

P(A ∩ B) **must not** = 0.

Example:

a Find the probability of drawing a card that is both a six and a heart (in other words, the six of hearts) from a 52-card pack.

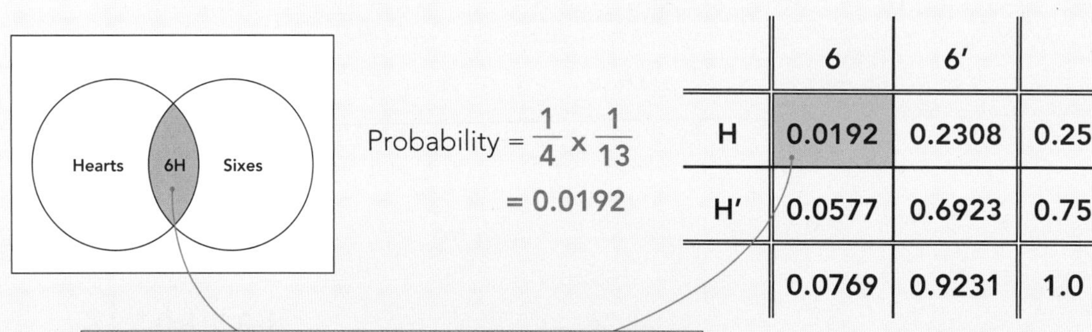

$$\text{Probability} = \frac{1}{4} \times \frac{1}{13}$$
$$= 0.0192$$

	6	6′	
H	0.0192	0.2308	0.25
H′	0.0577	0.6923	0.75
	0.0769	0.9231	1.0

Overlap ⇒ events are NOT mutually exclusive.

b Find the probability of drawing a heart or a six from a 52-card pack.

$$P(H \cup 6) = P(H) + P(6) - P(H \cap 6)$$
$$= 0.25 + 0.0769 - 0.0192$$
$$= 0.3077$$

In general: $P(A \cup B) = P(A) + P(B) - P(A \cap B)$
and
$P(A \cap B) \neq 0$

This is on your formula sheet.

PHOTOCOPYING OF THIS PAGE IS RESTRICTED UNDER LAW.
ISBN: 9780170389372

walkermaths

Cut along the lines, mix the pieces, and match each word piece with its definition. Then solve the example problems and find the word and definition that best fits each one.

Word	Definition	Example problems
Experimental probability	The probability obtained from an experiment or an observational study. 2	If 18 000 people were given a standardised test and 756 people refused to do it, what is the probability that a person did the test? B
Theoretical probability	The probability obtained from a model based on mathematical theory or observations about the behaviour of objects in an idealised world. 8	Calculate the probability of getting a total of 4 or 5 when two dice are thrown. E
Multiplication Principle	If there are p different ways of filling position 1, q different ways of filling position 2 and r different ways of filling position 3, then there are p x q x r ways of filling the three positions. 1	Six members of a chess team are seated randomly in a line for a photograph. Calculate the probability that the captain and the vice-captain are seated in the middle. G
Intersection	Where two or more events occur at the same time. 6	$P(S' \cup T) = 0.8$, $P(T') = 0.6$, $P(S') = 0.75$. Calculate $P(S \cap T)$. J
Disjoint events	Events that cannot both occur at the same time. 3	$P(B \cap A') = 0.35$, $P(A') = 0.9$, $P(B) = 0.45$. Calculate $P(A \cap B')$. A

PHOTOCOPYING OF THIS PAGE IS RESTRICTED UNDER LAW. ISBN: 9780170389372

Word	Definition	Example problems
Complementary events	An event where there are only two possible outcomes. 7	$P(G \cap H) = 0$, $P(G \cup H) = 1$, $P(H) = 0.34$. Calculate (G/H). F
Conditional probability	Where the probability of an event depends on the occurrence or non-occurrence of another event. 5	$P(Z') = 0.3$, $P(Y/Z') = 0.\dot{3}$, $P(Y \cap Z) = 0.65$. Calculate $P(Z/Y')$. H
Independent event	An event whose probability is not altered by the occurrence or non-occurrence of a second event. 9	$P(M/N) = P(M) = 0.45$, $P(M \cap N) = 0.1125$. Calculate $P(N)$. C
Absolute risk	The probability of something (bad) happening, given a certain condition. 10	The probability a person has a flu vaccination and catches the flu is 0.005. The probability a person doesn't have a flu vaccination and catches the flu is 0.155. Of the whole group, 21.5% were vaccinated. Calculate the probability that an unvaccinated person gets the flu. D
Relative risk	The risk of one event in relation to the risk of a second event. 4	The probability a person has a flu vaccination and catches the flu is 0.005. The probability a person doesn't have a flu vaccination and catches the flu is 0.155. Of the whole group, 21.5% were vaccinated. Calculate the probability that an unvaccinated person gets the flu compared with the probability that a vaccinated person gets the flu. I

ISBN: 9780170389372 PHOTOCOPYING OF THIS PAGE IS RESTRICTED UNDER LAW.

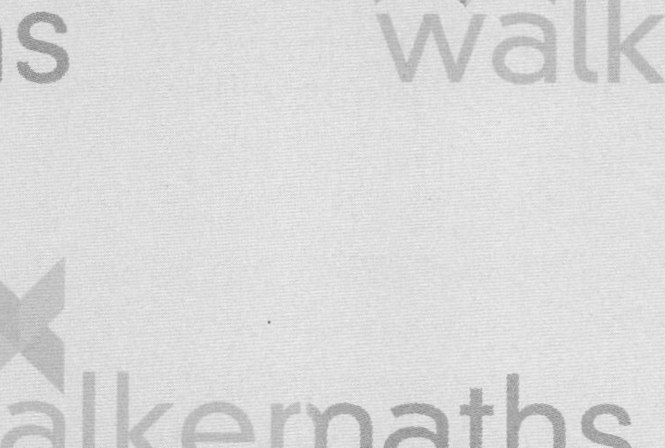

walkermaths

Complementary events (A and A′)

- Two events are complementary if their probabilities **add to 1**.
- These events are also mutually exclusive.
- This means that **one event or the other must occur**.
- If A is an event, then A′ (not A) is the **complementary** event.

The probability of A **or** A′: $P(A \cup A') = P(A) + P(A') = 1$

The probability of A **and** A′: $P(A \cap A') = 0$

$P(A) + P(A') = 1$

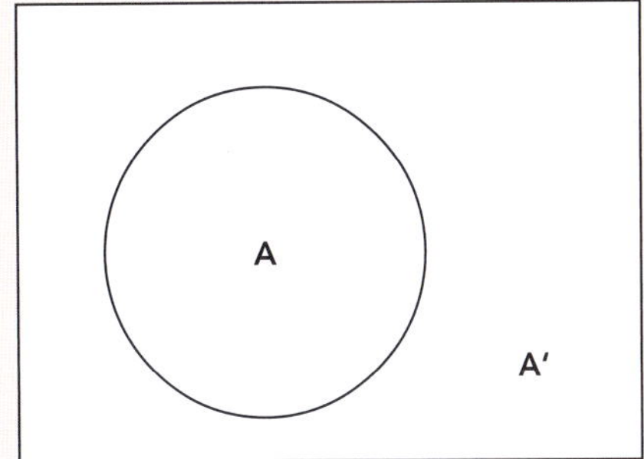

Example: Find the probability of picking a red card or a black card from a 52-card pack.

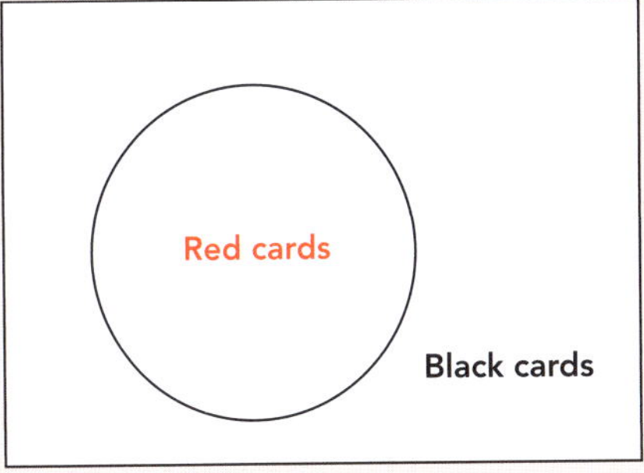

$$\begin{aligned} P(\text{red or black}) &= P(R) + P(B) \\ &= 0.5 + 0.5 \\ &= 1 \end{aligned}$$

In general: $P(A) + P(A') = P(A \cup A') = 1$

and

$P(A \cap A') = 0$

Note: Complementary events **are** mutually exclusive.
However, mutually exclusive events **are not necessarily** complementary.

ISBN: 9780170389372 PHOTOCOPYING OF THIS PAGE IS RESTRICTED UNDER LAW.

Conditional probability

- Where the probability of an event (A) is **altered by the occurrence of another event** (B), we say the probabilities are **conditional**.
- This is written as **P(A/B)**.
- In words this is 'the probability that A occurs **given that** B has occurred'.

These are some ways of expressing the **same** conditional probability, **P(A/B)**, where event A is 'a student is in the arm wrestling team' and event B is 'a student is in the bouldering team':

> 'Calculate the probability that a student is in the arm wrestling team **given that** the student is in the bouldering team.'
> '**Given that** a student is in the bouldering team, calculate the probability the student is in the arm wrestling team.'
> 'Calculate the probability that a student is in the arm wrestling team **if** the student is in the bouldering team.'
> '**If** a student is in the bouldering team, calculate the probability the student is in the arm wrestling team.'
> 'Calculate the probability that a student who is in the bouldering team is also in the arm wrestling team.'

It is useful to consider a probability tree:

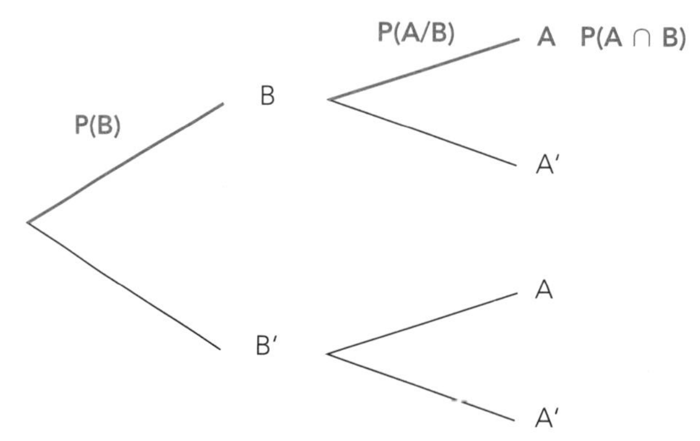

$\therefore$ **P(A ∩ B) = P(B) x P(A/B)**

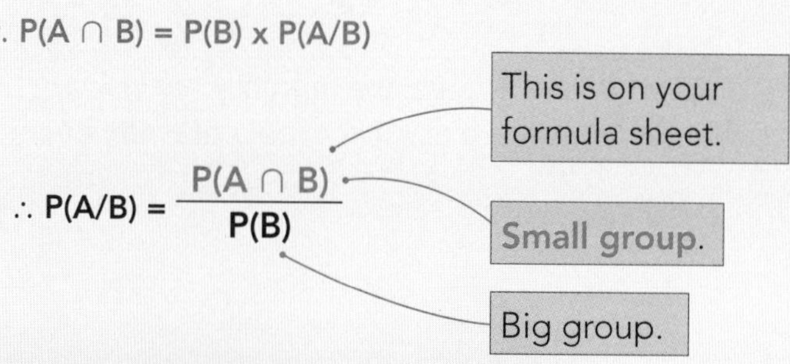

$$\therefore P(A/B) = \frac{P(A \cap B)}{P(B)}$$

Order is important: P(A/B) ≠ P(B/A)

PHOTOCOPYING OF THIS PAGE IS RESTRICTED UNDER LAW. ISBN: 9780170389372

Example: Consider the subject choices of some Year 13 students.

a The probability that a student takes Art is 0.15, and the probability that a student takes both Art and Design is $0.08\dot{3}$. Calculate the probability that a student takes Design, given that he or she takes Art.

Step 1: Write in symbols what you know. $P(A) = 0.15$ and $P(D \cap A) = 0.08\dot{3}$

Step 2: Write down what you need to know. $P(D/A)$

Step 3: Use the formula.

$$P(D/A) = \frac{P(D \cap A)}{P(A)}$$

Use appropriate letters.

$$= \frac{0.08\dot{3}}{0.15}$$

$$= 0.\dot{5}$$

Alternative method: Use reasoning and a probability table (you have been doing this in previous sections of the book).

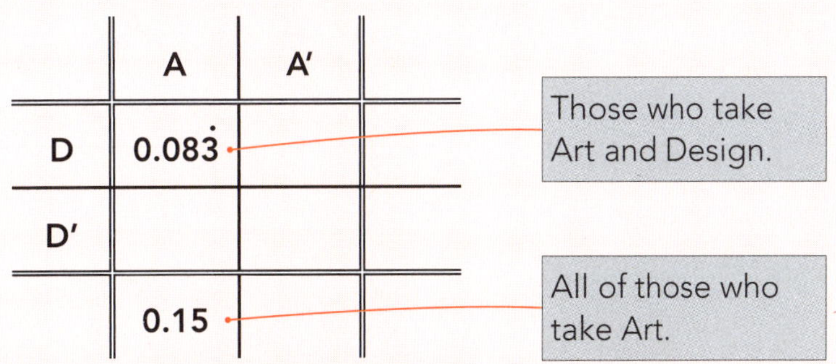

	A	A′	
D	$0.08\dot{3}$		
D′			
	0.15		

$$P(D/A) = \frac{\text{Those who take Design and Art}}{\text{Those who take just Art}}$$

$$= \frac{0.08\dot{3}}{0.15} = 0.\dot{5}$$

Alternative method: Use a probability tree.

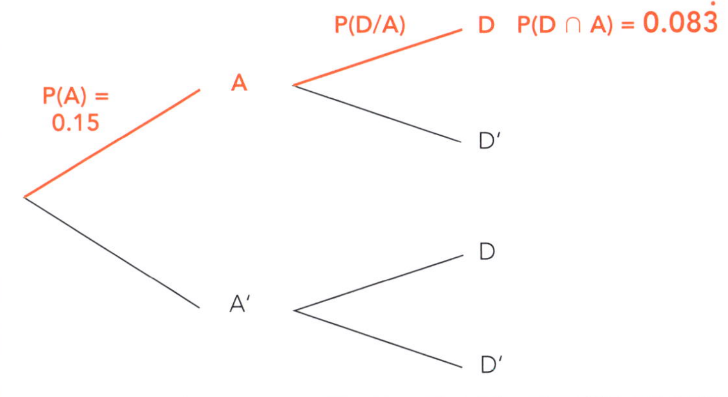

$$P(D/A) = \frac{0.08\dot{3}}{0.15}$$

$$= 0.\dot{5}$$

Example: Consider the subject choices of some Year 13 students.

b The probability that a student doesn't take Art is 0.85. The probability that a student takes Design, given that he or she doesn't take Art, is $0.1\dot{6}$. Calculate the probability that a student takes Design but not Art.

Step 1: Write in symbols what you know. $P(A') = 0.85$ and $P(D/A') = 0.1\dot{6}$

Step 2: Write down what you need to know. $P(D \cap A')$

Step 3: Use the formula.

$$P(D/A') = \frac{P(D \cap A')}{P(A')}$$

Use appropriate letters.

$$\therefore P(D \cap A') = P(D/A') \times P(A') = 0.1\dot{6} \times 0.85 = 0.142$$

Alternative method: Use reasoning and a probability table.

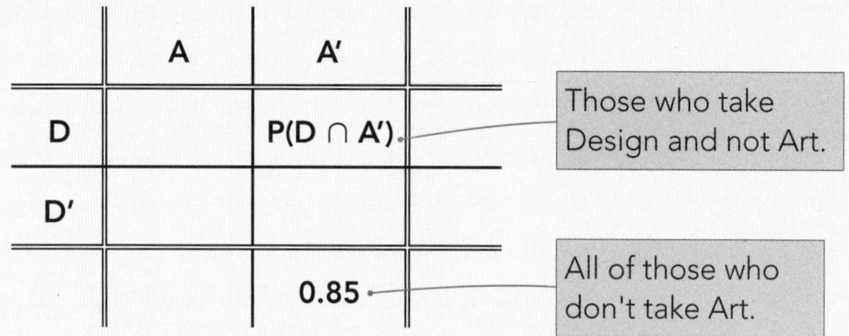

	A	A'	
D		**P(D ∩ A')**	
D'			
		0.85	

$$P(D/A') = \frac{P(D \cap A')}{0.85} = 0.1\dot{6}$$

$$\therefore P(D \cap A') = 0.85 \times 0.1\dot{6} = 0.142$$

Alternative method: Use a probability tree.

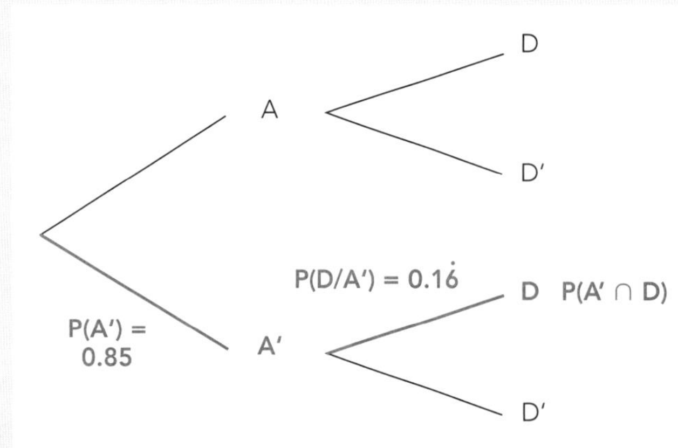

$$P(D \cap A') = P(A' \cap D) = 0.85 \times 0.1\dot{6} = 0.142$$

PHOTOCOPYING OF THIS PAGE IS RESTRICTED UNDER LAW.
ISBN: 9780170389372

Putting it together

Answer the following questions.

1 Event A is 'a student owns a pink phone'.
Event B is 'a student is a boy'.
Write down the correct expression for each of the following probabilities.

		P(A/B) or P(B/A)?
a	The probability that a student is a boy given that the student has a pink phone.	
b	The probability that the student has a pink phone if the student is a boy.	
c	The probability that a boy owns a pink phone.	
d	The probability that a student is a boy if he owns a pink phone.	
e	The probability that a student owns a pink phone, given that the student is a boy.	
f	The probability that a pink phone owner is a boy.	

2 $P(A) = 0.8$, $P(B) = 0.5$ and $P(A \cap B) = 0.3$.

a Calculate $P(A/B)$.

____

b Calculate $P(B/A)$.

____

3 $P(A) = 0.5$, $P(B) = 0.6$ and $P(B/A) = 0.4$.

a Calculate $P(A \cap B)$.

____

b Calculate $P(A/B)$.

____

4 $P(A') = 0.65$, $P(B) = 0.45$ and $P(A' \cap B') = 0.3$.

a Calculate $P(B')$.

____

b Calculate $P(A'/B')$.

____

ISBN: 9780170389372 PHOTOCOPYING OF THIS PAGE IS RESTRICTED UNDER LAW.

5 $P(A \cap B) = 0.4$, $P(A/B) = 0.8$, and $P(A) = 0.6$.

a Calculate P(B).

b Calculate P(B/A).

c Calculate $P(A \cup B)$.

6 $P(A \cap B) = 0.1$, $P(A/B) = 0.25$ and $P(B/A) = 0.2$.

a Calculate P(A).

b Calculate P(B).

c Calculate $P(A \cup B)'$.

7 $P(B) = 0.4$, $P(A') = 0.3$ and $P(B \cap A') = 0.12$.

a Complete the probability table.

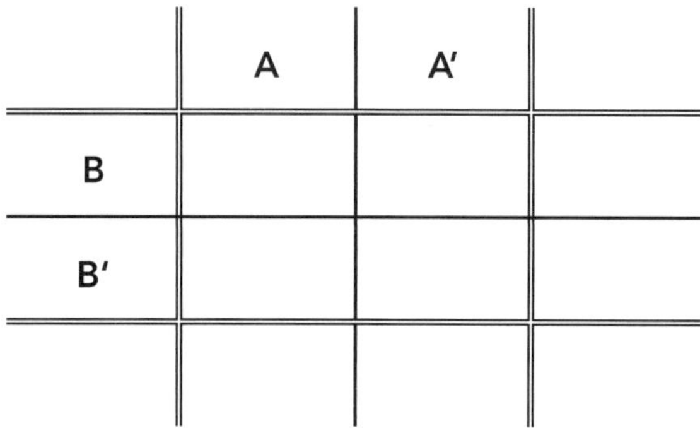

	A	A'	
B			
B'			

b Are events A and B mutually exclusive? Justify your answer.

c What is the probability that both A and B′ occur?

d Calculate P(A/B).

PHOTOCOPYING OF THIS PAGE IS RESTRICTED UNDER LAW.
ISBN: 9780170389372

8 P(A′) = 0.8, P(B′) = 0.55 and P(A′ ∩ B′) = 0.35.

a Complete the probability table.

	A	**A′**	
B			
B′			

b Are events A and B mutually exclusive? Justify your answer.

____

c What is the probability that both A and B′ occur?

____

d Calculate P(A′/B).

____

e Explain the meaning of your previous answer.

____

____

9 P(A) = 0.35, P(B) = 0.7 and P(A ∪ B) = 0.95.

a Complete the probability table.

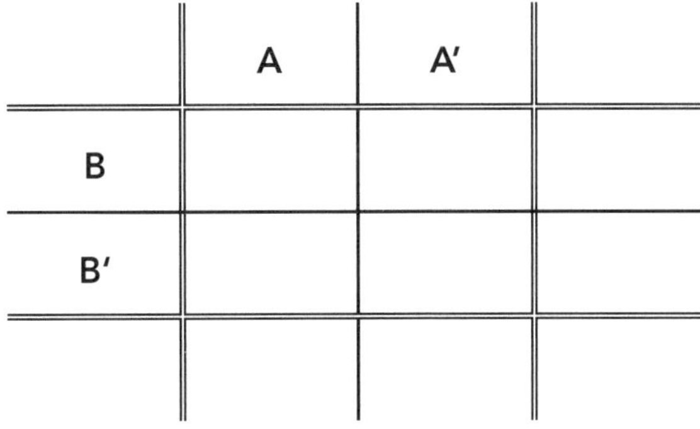

	A	**A′**	
B			
B′			

b Are events A and B mutually exclusive? Justify your answer.

____

c What is the probability that both A′ and B occur?

____

d Calculate P(A/B).

____

10 The school formal is planned for the night before the grand final of the squash competition. Of Year 13 students, 89% are going to the formal; 12% of Year 13 students play squash; 4% of students do not intend to go to the formal, and they don't play squash.

a Complete the probability table.

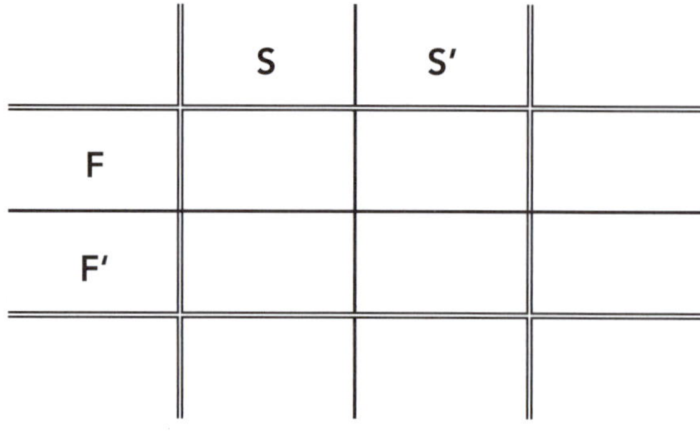

	S	S′	
F			
F′			

b Are events 'a student is going to the formal' and 'a student plays squash' mutually exclusive? Justify your answer.

c What is the probability that a student plays squash given that he or she is going to the formal?

d Calculate the probability that a squash player is going to the formal.

11 A random check of a large number of cars revealed that 96% were warranted. Of those that were warranted, 94% were registered. Cars were twice as likely to be registered given they were warranted, than if they were unwarranted.

a Complete the probability tree.

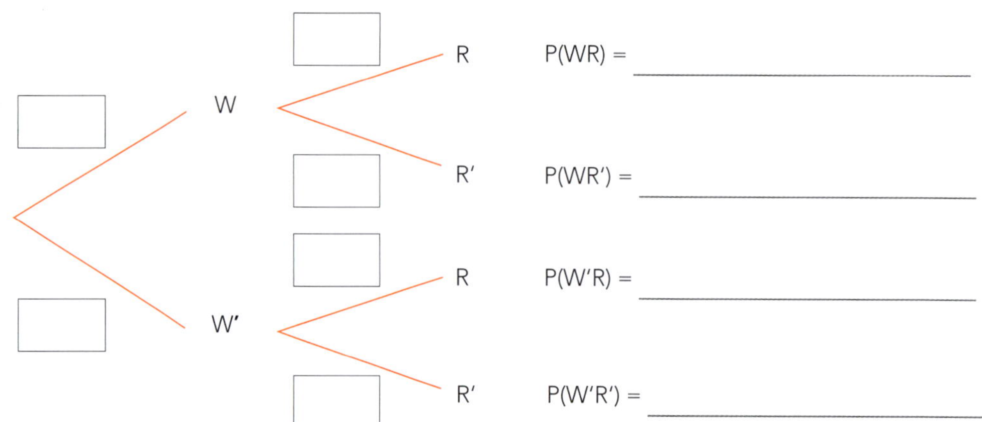

b Calculate the probability that a car was registered.

PHOTOCOPYING OF THIS PAGE IS RESTRICTED UNDER LAW.
ISBN: 9780170389372

Independent events

- Events are **independent** if the occurrence of one event makes **no difference** to the probability of a second event.
  Example: The events A, 'a student's phone is a Samsung', and B, 'a student is a boy', are probably **independent**.
  This means that **P(A) = P(A/B)**.

  The probability that a student's phone is a Samsung will probably be the same, whether or not it is owned by a boy.

- Applying this to a probability tree:

  Independent ⇒ **P(B/A) = P(B)**

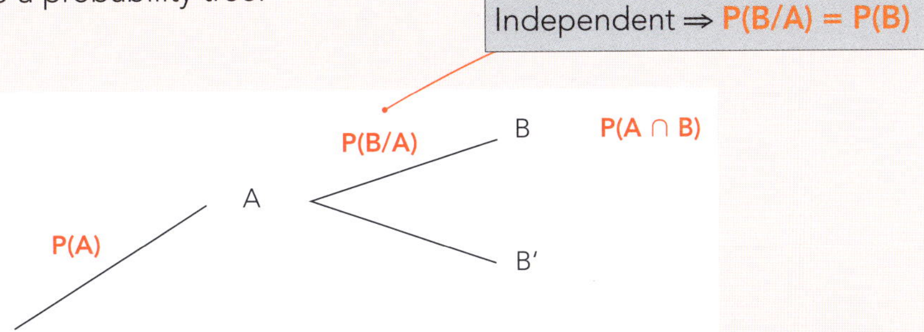

∴ P(A ∩ B) = P(A) x P(B)

So events are independent if: P(A) = P(A/B) or P(A ∩ B) = P(A) x P(B)

- Events are **dependent** (or **not independent**) if the occurrence of one **changes** the probability that the other occurs.
  Example: The events A' a student's phone is pink' and B 'a student is a boy' are probably **dependent**.
  This means that **P(events A) ≠ P(A/B).**

  The probability that a student's phone is pink is different if it is owned by a boy.

Examples:

1 Consider the subject choices of some Year 13 students. The probability that a student takes Art is 0.15, and the probability that a student takes Design is also 0.15. The probability that a student takes both Art and Design is $0.08\dot{3}$. Are these events independent? Explain the meaning of your answer.

Hint: Write in symbols what you know: P(A) = 0.15, P(D) = 0.15 and P(A ∩ D) = $0.08\dot{3}$.

Independence ⇒ ***P(A ∩ D) = P(A) x P(D)***

P(A ∩ D) = $0.08\dot{3}$

P(A) x P(D) = 0.15^2 *= 0.0225*

∴ P(A ∩ D) ≠ P(A) x P(D)

∴ Events A and D are not independent.

Because P(A ∩ D) **>** *P(A) x P(D), students are* ***more*** *likely than expected to do both Art and Design.*

ISBN: 9780170389372 PHOTOCOPYING OF THIS PAGE IS RESTRICTED UNDER LAW.

2 The table shows the numbers of Year 13 students who play a sport and the numbers who study Chemistry.

	S	S′
C	16	26
C′	71	53

Are the events 'a Year 13 student plays a sport' and 'a Year 13 student takes Chemistry' independent? Explain the meaning of your answer.

Step 1: Add the totals to the table.

	S	S′	Totals
C	16	26	42
C′	71	53	124
Totals	87	79	166

Step 2: ***Either***

$$P(C) = 0.2530$$
$$P(C/S) = 0.1839$$
$$\therefore P(C) \neq P(C/S)$$

Because P(C) ≠ P(C/S), the events are not independent, and because P(C) > P(C/S), Year 13 students who play a sport are less likely to take Chemistry than expected.

Or

$$P(S) = 0.5241$$
$$P(S/C) = 0.3810$$
$$\therefore P(S) \neq P(S/C)$$

Because P(S) ≠ P(S/C), the events are not independent, and because P(S) > P(S/C), Year 13 students who take Chemistry are less likely than expected to play a sport.

Or

$$P(C) \times P(S) = 0.2530 \times 0.5241 = 0.1326$$
$$P(C \cap S) = 0.0964$$
$$\therefore P(C) \times P(S) \neq P(C \cap S)$$

Because P(C) x P(S) ≠ P(C ∩ S) the events are not independent, and because P(C) x P(S) > P(C ∩ S), students are less likely than expected to both take Chemistry and play a sport.

PHOTOCOPYING OF THIS PAGE IS RESTRICTED UNDER LAW.
ISBN: 9780170389372

Answer the following questions.

1 State whether the events in the following questions are independent or not, and justify your decision.

a P(A) = 0.4, P(B) = 0.3 and P(A ∩ B) = 0.2

b P(A) = 0.2, P(B) = 0.6 and P(A/B) = 0.3

c P(A) = 0.5, P(B) = 0.2 and P(A ∩ B) = 0.1

d P(A) = 0.75, P(B) = 0.45 and P(B/A) = 0.45

2 State whether the following events are independent or not, and justify your decision. You may need to complete the probability table.

a P(A) = 0.3, P(B) = 0.2 and P(A ∪ B) = 0.44

	A	A′	
B			
B′			

b P(A) = 0.6, P(B) = 0.8 and P(A′ ∩ B′) = 0

	A	A′	
B			
B′			

c P(A) = 0.6, P(B) = 0.75 and P(A′ ∪ B) = 0.85

	A	A′	
B			
B′			

ISBN: 9780170389372 PHOTOCOPYING OF THIS PAGE IS RESTRICTED UNDER LAW.

3 P(A) = 0.6 and P(A ∩ B) = 0.42 and events A and B are independent events.

a Complete the table.

b What is the probability that either A or B occurs?

c Calculate P(B/A).

	A	A'	
B			
B'			

4 The probability that a Year 13 student studies Level 3 English is 0.35. The probability that a Year 13 student studies Level 3 English and plays a sport is 0.14. If these events are independent:

a Complete the table.

b Calculate the probability that a Year 13 student studies Level 3 English or plays a sport.

	E	E'	
S			
S'			

c What is the probability that a Year 13 student plays a sport given that he or she takes Level 3 English?

5 For a group of Year 13 students, 35% take Level 3 English and 15% take Level 3 History. If 39% take one or more of these subjects:

a What is the probability that a student takes both?

b Are these two events independent? Justify your answer.

 PHOTOCOPYING OF THIS PAGE IS RESTRICTED UNDER LAW. ISBN: 9780170389372

6 The table shows the results from a survey of 1000 people. The survey asked whether people drank alcohol (event D) and whether they smoked cigarettes (event S).

	D	D′
S	204	7
S′	658	131

a Find the probability that a person was a smoker, given that they were a drinker.

b Find the probability that a smoker drinks.

c Are the events 'a person is a drinker' and 'a person is a smoker' independent? Justify your answer.

d Explain what your answer to **c** means in this context.

7 A dairy owner records whether his customers are under or over 40 years old, and whether or not they buy a newspaper. The results are shown in the table.

	N	N′
≥ 40	150	173
< 40	54	623

a Are the events 'a customer buys a newspaper' and 'a customer is under 40 years old' independent? Justify your answer.

b Explain what your answer to **a** means in this context.

ISBN: 9780170389372 PHOTOCOPYING OF THIS PAGE IS RESTRICTED UNDER LAW.

8 A car sales company kept data on the prices of cars sold and how long each car took to be sold.

Event		A	B	C	Totals
		< $10 000	$10 000 – $30 000	> $30 000	
R	**< 20 days**	35	45	9	**89**
S	**20–50 days**	25	41	17	**83**
T	**> 50 days**	3	22	14	**39**
	Totals	**63**	**108**	**40**	**211**

a Calculate the probability that a car that sold for more than $30 000 was sold in fewer than 20 days.

b Calculate the probability that a car that sold for between $10 000 and $30 000 was sold in 50 days or less.

c Calculate the probability that a car that sold in 50 days or less was sold for between $10 000 and $30 000.

d Are the events A (a car sold for less than $10 000) and R (a car sold in fewer than 20 days) independent?

e Explain what the previous answer means.

f Are the events A (a car sold for less than $10 000) and S (a car sold in between 20 and 50 days) independent?

g Explain what the previous answer means.

PHOTOCOPYING OF THIS PAGE IS RESTRICTED UNDER LAW. ISBN: 9780170389372

Risk

- The word 'risk' refers to the probability of something bad happening. Nobody ever talks about the risk of winning Lotto. However, the risks of car crashes or catching a disease are commonly discussed.
- The term "likelihood ratio" is sometimes used instead of "risk".
- There are two types of risk that you need to be able to calculate.

1 Absolute risk

- Absolute risk is the **probability** of something (bad) happening, given a certain condition.

Example: A new drug was trialled on 1000 patients: 500 were given the new drug and 500 were given a placebo. Of the 500 given the new drug, 63 developed a rash, while 18 of those given the placebo developed a rash.

Group given drug: Absolute risk of rash $= \frac{63}{500} = 0.126$

Group given placebo: Absolute risk of rash $= \frac{18}{500} = 0.036$

These are often conditional probabilities.

2 Relative risk

- This is the risk of one event **divided by** the risk of a second event.
- Unlike probability, relative risk **can** take values that are **greater than 1**.

$$\textbf{Relative risk} = \frac{\textbf{Absolute risk of event A}}{\textbf{Absolute risk of event B}}$$

Relative risk > 1 ⇒ The risk is greater for event A than for event B.

Example: Relative risk of a rash with the drug, compared with the placebo

$$= \frac{0.126}{0.036} = 3.5$$

This means that patients given the drug are 3.5 times as likely to experience a rash than those given the placebo.

Relative risk = 1 ⇒ The risk is the same for both events.

Relative risk < 1 ⇒ The risk is less for event A than event B.

Example: Relative risk of a rash with the placebo, compared with the drug

$$= \frac{0.036}{0.126} = 0.2857$$

This means that patients given the placebo are 0.2857 times as likely to experience a rash compared with those given the drug.

ISBN: 9780170389372 PHOTOCOPYING OF THIS PAGE IS RESTRICTED UNDER LAW.

Example: A trial was done on 1000 sheep in order to determine the effectiveness of a vaccine to protect the sheep against a disease. The vaccine was given to 600 sheep, and the remaining 400 were not vaccinated. Records were kept of how many sheep got the disease.

	Disease	No disease	Totals
Vaccinated	39	561	**600**
Unvaccinated	87	313	**400**
Totals	**126**	**874**	**1000**

a Calculate the absolute risk that a sheep got the disease.

$$\text{Absolute risk} = \frac{\text{Total number that have disease}}{\text{Total number of sheep}} = \frac{126}{1000} = 0.126$$

b Calculate the absolute risk that an unvaccinated sheep got the disease.

$$\text{Absolute risk} = \frac{\text{Number of unvaccinated sheep that got disease}}{\text{Number of unvaccinated sheep}} = \frac{87}{400} = 0.2175$$

c Calculate the absolute risk that a vaccinated sheep got the disease.

$$\text{Absolute risk} = \frac{\text{Number of vaccinated sheep that got disease}}{\text{Number of vaccinated sheep}} = \frac{39}{600} = 0.065$$

d Calculate the relative risk that an unvaccinated sheep gets the disease, compared with a vaccinated sheep.

$$\text{Relative risk} = \frac{\text{Probability of getting disease if unvaccinated}}{\text{Probability of getting disease if vaccinated}} = \frac{0.2175}{0.065} = 3.346$$

e Explain what your result means.

An unvaccinated sheep is more than three times as likely to get the disease than a vaccinated sheep.

f The farmer wanted to use the absolute risk of a vaccinated sheep getting the disease in order to estimate the number of vaccinated sheep likely to get this disease in the following year. Discuss what else the farmer should consider to estimate this risk.

Weather varies from year to year, and this might alter the risk of getting the disease. Different paddocks are likely to have different conditions — shelter, shade, grass type, etc. The farmer would need to consider whether there are other sheep that might transmit the disease in nearby paddocks. The density of sheep in a paddock is likely to affect the risk of getting the disease.

PHOTOCOPYING OF THIS PAGE IS RESTRICTED UNDER LAW.
ISBN: 9780170389372

Try these questions.

1 A farmer split his flock of ewes into two groups. One group of 400 ewes was given extra feed during autumn, and the other group of 250 ewes was not given extra feed. He then recorded the number of ewes in each group that had multiple births (twins or triplets). Of those given extra feed, 137 had multiple births; of those that didn't have extra feed, 46 had multiple births.

a Complete the following table using the information given.

	Multiple births	Single births	Totals
Extra feed			
No extra feed			
Totals			

b Calculate the absolute risk that a ewe has a multiple birth.

c Calculate the absolute risk that a ewe that was fed extra had a multiple birth.

d Calculate the absolute risk that a ewe that was not fed extra had a multiple birth.

e Calculate the relative risk of a ewe that was fed extra having a multiple birth, compared with a ewe that was not fed extra.

f Explain what this means.

g The farmer wanted to use the absolute risk that a ewe that was fed extra had a multiple birth in order to estimate the number of ewes having extra feed that are likely to have a multiple birth in the following year. Discuss what else the farmer should consider in order to estimate this risk.

ISBN: 9780170389372
PHOTOCOPYING OF THIS PAGE IS RESTRICTED UNDER LAW.

2 A long-term study on 1000 people was performed. Of the 400 smokers, 220 developed lung cancer. Of the 600 who did not smoke, 32 developed lung cancer.

a Complete the following table using the information given.

	Lung cancer	No lung cancer	Totals
Smokers			
Non-smokers			
Totals			

b Calculate the absolute risk that a person develops lung cancer.

c Calculate the absolute risk that a smoker develops lung cancer.

d Calculate the absolute risk that a non-smoker develops lung cancer.

e Calculate the relative risk that a smoker develops lung cancer, compared with a non-smoker.

f Explain what this means.

g Another study of lung cancer incidence examined 500 people. How many would you expect to have lung cancer? Would you be surprised if 132 had lung cancer? Why?

 PHOTOCOPYING OF THIS PAGE IS RESTRICTED UNDER LAW. ISBN: 9780170389372

3 A large amount of data was collected in order to determine the effectiveness of aspirin in preventing heart attacks: 10 000 people were given aspirin, and of those, 135 had heart attacks, the remaining 8000 people were given a placebo, and of those, 175 had heart attacks.

a Complete the following table using the information given.

	Heart attack	No heart attack	Totals
Aspirin			
Placebo			
Totals			

b Calculate the absolute risk that a person has a heart attack.

c Calculate the absolute risk that a person who takes aspirin has a heart attack.

d Calculate the absolute risk that a person who takes the placebo has a heart attack.

e Calculate the relative risk that a person who takes aspirin has a heart attack, compared with a person who takes a placebo.

f Explain what this means.

g The investigator wanted to use the absolute risk that a person who takes aspirin will have a heart attack to predict the numbers of people in another group who will have heart attacks. Discuss what else the investigator should consider in order to estimate this risk.

ISBN: 9780170389372
PHOTOCOPYING OF THIS PAGE IS RESTRICTED UNDER LAW.

4 Some people were very ill after the school formal (and not for the reasons you are thinking of!). Of the 276 students who ate chicken, 172 were ill. Of the 104 students who didn't eat the chicken, 12 were ill.

a Complete the following table using the information given.

	Ate chicken	Did not eat chicken	Totals
Ill			
Not ill			
Totals			

b Calculate the absolute risk that a person was ill.

c Calculate the absolute risk that a person who had eaten chicken was ill.

d Calculate the absolute risk that a person who had not eaten chicken was ill.

e Calculate the relative risk that person who had eaten chicken was ill, compared with a person who hadn't eaten chicken.

f Explain what this means.

g Another formal on the same night used the same caterers. There were 465 people at this formal. If the same chicken dish were served, how many would you expect to be ill? Would you be surprised if 143 were ill? Why?

PHOTOCOPYING OF THIS PAGE IS RESTRICTED UNDER LAW.
ISBN: 9780170389372

5 For several years records were kept of the number of drivers who got speeding tickets in a particular area, and the total number of licensed drivers living in the area. The data is shown below.

	2013	2014	2015
Number of licensed drivers living in area	53 412	56 014	57 344
Number of those with speeding offences	2580	3193	3498

a Which year had the greatest overall risk of getting a speeding ticket for a licensed driver who lived in the area? Support your answer with calculations.

b How does the risk of getting a speeding ticket for a licensed driver who lives in the area in 2015 compare with the risk in 2013?

c Give reasons why the risks calculated in **a** are only estimates of the true overall risk of getting a speeding ticket for people driving in the area.

d A driver wanted to use the overall risk of getting a speeding ticket during 2015 to estimate the risk of getting a speeding ticket in the area during 2016. Discuss reasons why his or her estimate may not be particularly accurate.

ISBN: 9780170389372 PHOTOCOPYING OF THIS PAGE IS RESTRICTED UNDER LAW.

6 Flying on commercial flights is often perceived as being risky compared with travelling in a car. In a particular country during 2015, 0.212 people died due to crashes during commercial flights for every 100 million kilometres travelled; while travelling in a car, 1.473 people died due to crashes for every 100 million kilometres travelled.

a Calculate the relative risk of travelling by car, compared with travelling on commercial flights.

b Explain what this means.

c The transport agency in the country wanted to use the relative risk that you calculated in **a** in order to predict the equivalent risk for 2016. Explain why this prediction may not be particularly accurate.

7 Tests for medical conditions are not usually 100% accurate. One in 1000 people have a particular blood condition. The test for it gives a true positive result in 95% of cases, and a true negative result in 99% of cases.

a Calculate the risk of having this blood condition if you tested positive.

b Explain what this means.

c Calculate the risk that you do not have this blood condition, given that you tested negative.

d Explain what your last answer means.

PHOTOCOPYING OF THIS PAGE IS RESTRICTED UNDER LAW.
ISBN: 9780170389372

Sampling and randomness

Sampling

- When collecting data, we nearly always have to take a **sample** from our **population**.
- We then use sample data to make **inferences** about the population.

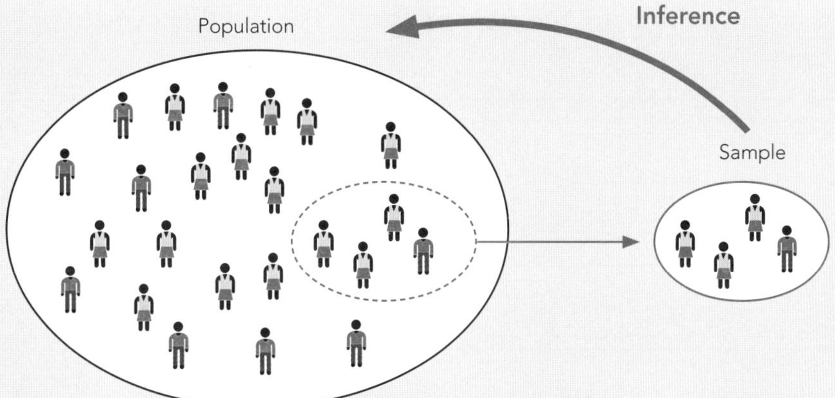

Inference is the process of drawing a conclusion about the population, based on what is discovered in the sample.

There are two important questions to ask when considering data from a sample:

1 Is the sample big enough?

- A sample of 30 is generally considered enough for most purposes.
- However, the bigger the sample, the more confidence you can have of your findings.

The bigger the sample, the more confidence you can have of your findings.

2 Is the data biased?

- Bias occurs when some members of the population are more likely than others to be selected for the sample, so the sample does not truly represent the population.

Examples:

- Ringing a radio station, filling in a form in a magazine or going to a website to give feedback: these are called 'self-selected' samples because the subject decides whether they will be sampled. Only those with an interest in the topic of the survey will be in the sample.
- The survey in the mall: this collects data only from those who go to malls, those who have time to answer, and there is an element of self-selection.
- Telephone surveys: these are done on land lines, so mostly older people and people who don't often move house are surveyed. These also tend to be self-selected because many people choose not to respond.

A truly random sample will be unbiased.

ISBN: 9780170389372 PHOTOCOPYING OF THIS PAGE IS RESTRICTED UNDER LAW.

Randomness

- A **random** sample is a sample in which every individual in the population has an **equal probability of being selected**.
- Randomness in probability means that events are **independent** of each other: a previous outcome does not affect the probability that an event will occur.

Answer the following questions.

1 In the box below, write down the results (H or T) that you **think** you might get if you tossed a coin 50 times.

2 Now toss a coin 50 times and record your results in the box below.

3 Compare your results. Look at other people's results. What do you notice?

PHOTOCOPYING OF THIS PAGE IS RESTRICTED UNDER LAW.
ISBN: 9780170389372

Simulation

Simulations **imitate** the **true probability situation** using devices such as dice, cards, random numbers, etc. Simulations can be used to find probabilities when:

- a precise mathematical model is not available to calculate probabilities
- applying a mathematical model is difficult, time consuming or expensive.

For a simulation to produce accurate results:

1 The model on which the simulation is based must accurately reflect the real situation.
2 The simulation must be repeated many times.

Example: A company promotes its chocolate milk by claiming that one bottle in five will have a prize-winning number under the cap of the bottle. Alfred and his friends bought 15 bottles between them during the term, and two prizes were won. Alfred maintains that they should have won three prizes for buying 15 bottles.

a Calculate the observed (experimental) probability of winning two prizes from 15 bottles.

The observed (experimental) probability of winning two prizes from 15 bottles

$$= \frac{2}{15} = 0.1\dot{3}$$

b Alfred wrote down the theoretical (model estimate) for the probability of winning a prize, and used it to calculate the expected number of prizes from 15 bottles. Show how he did this.

The theoretical (model estimate) for the probability of winning $= \frac{1}{5} = 0.2$

$$\Rightarrow \text{Expected number of prizes from 15 bottles} = \frac{1}{5} \times 15 = 3$$

In order to test this, Alfred performed a simulation.

- He used random numbers and let 1 and 2 represent a prize-winning number.
- He selected sets of 15 random numbers.
- For each set of 15 numbers, he recorded the number of 1s and 2s.
- He set up his computer to repeat this simulation 1000 times.
- He created a table to show his results:

Number of 1s and 2s	0	1	2	3	4	5	6	7	8
Frequency	34	137	236	249	188	99	43	11	3

c Based on his simulation results, what can Alfred conclude about whether or not one bottle in every five wins a prize and the likelihood of winning exactly three prizes?

From his simulation, the probability of winning two prizes from 15 bottles $= \frac{236}{1000} = 0.236.$

This is considerably larger than his observed (experimental) probability of 0.13, which suggests that the number of bottles with prizes may be less than one in five.

However Alfred and his friends bought only 15 bottles. This is quite a small number, so they may have won just two prizes due to chance. If they wanted to know if one bottle in five really does have a prize-winning number, they would need to buy lots more bottles. The simulation also shows him that it was likely that he would not win exactly three prizes. Only in 24.9% of sets of 15 bottles would exactly three prizes be won.

ISBN: 9780170389372 PHOTOCOPYING OF THIS PAGE IS RESTRICTED UNDER LAW.

Answer the following questions.

1 Consider the first digit in a list of the population sizes of the world's 200 most populous countries. For example, on a day in July 2016, New Zealand's population was 4 697 616, so the leading digit is 4.

a Write down what you would expect for the theoretical probability that a particular digit (e.g. 4) leads the population of a country, remembering that populations cannot start with a zero. ____________________

b Sean performed a simulation using the above answer. He used random numbers, ignoring all the zeros, and he did it 50 times. His results are shown below.

Number	1	2	3	4	5	6	7	8	9
Frequency	4	7	8	4	4	6	3	6	8

He concluded that the most likely leading digits were 3 and 9. Comment on his conclusion.

____

____

____

c Tracey performed the same simulation 1000 times and got the following results.

Number	1	2	3	4	5	6	7	8	9
Frequency	109	111	113	109	104	117	112	110	115

Suggest a conclusion that Tracey could come to for this simulation.

____

____

____

d The table below lists the actual frequencies of the leading digits of the populations of the world's 200 most populous countries. Complete the table to show the observed probabilities that each digit will be the leading digit of a population.

Number	1	2	3	4	5	6	7	8	9
Frequency	70	32	25	23	15	12	7	9	7
Probability	0.35								

e Comment on the assumption made in **a**.

____

____

____

Note: If you want to discover more about this, research Benford's Law.

PHOTOCOPYING OF THIS PAGE IS RESTRICTED UNDER LAW.
ISBN: 9780170389372

2 Ben and Meg are both collecting cards from packets of a popular cereal. There are four different cards, and each box contains one card. According to the makers of the cereal, the probabilities of getting each card are the same.

Ben thinks that the chance of collecting one of each card by buying six packets of cereal should be at least 0.5. Amy thinks that is unlikely, because it could take many more packets to collect the set.

a In order to decide who is right without buying lots of packets of cereal, they perform a simulation. They select all the aces, twos, threes and fours from a pack of cards, shuffle them, and draw cards with replacement, until they have drawn one of each number. They record the number of cards drawn before getting each full set.

i Were they correct to draw the cards with replacement in this situation? Explain.

ii They repeated their simulation 30 times. Their results are shown in the table. Complete the table to show the experimental probabilities for each situation.

Number of cards → full set	4	5	6	> 6
Frequency	3	6	5	16
Probability				

iii Because the outcome was close (a total probability of $0.4\dot{6}$ for completing the set in six or fewer packets), they set up a computer to do the simulation 1000 of times. Complete the table to show the experimental probabilities for each situation.

Number of cards → full set	4	5	6	> 6
Frequency	94	142	147	617
Probability				

iv Was Ben correct in thinking that the chance of collecting one of each card by buying six packets of cereal is at least 0.5? Justify your answer.

b In their second simulation, the experimental probability for getting a full set of cards by buying four packets of cereal was almost exactly equal to the theoretical probability.

Show how you could calculate the theoretical probability of getting all four cards from just four packets of cereal.

c Show that the probability of getting the complete set after buying five packets of cereal is 0.1406 (4 dp).

d Complete the probability table. The probability of getting a complete set after six packets of cereal is given to you.

Number of cards → full set	4	5	6	> 6
Probability			0.1465	

e How could Ben and Meg increase their chances for getting all four cards after buying six packets of cereal each?

f The true probability of collecting one of each card by buying just four packets of cereal is actually significantly less than 0.0938. What is the most likely explanation for this?

PHOTOCOPYING OF THIS PAGE IS RESTRICTED UNDER LAW.
ISBN: 9780170389372

3 A farmer bought a flock of 150 female goats. The seller promised him that about $\frac{1}{6}$ of this flock would produce twins each year, and the rest would produce single kids; triplets were extremely rare. The farmer kept a record of the breeding success for every goat for four years.

At the end of this period 98 goats had produced just four kids (no twins) and 44 goats had produced five kids each (one set of twins). He suspected that these numbers were too high if the probability of twins really was $\frac{1}{6}$. He was not confident that he could correctly calculate the expected numbers of goats that should have four or five kids if the probability of twins was $\frac{1}{6}$, so he designed a simulation to help.

He tossed four dice at a time, and recorded the number of sixes appearing in each set of four. Getting a six represented a goat having twins. He set up his computer to repeat this simulation 1000 times. His results are shown in the table.

Number of kids	4	5	6	7	8
Frequency	485	384	117	13	1

a What conclusion can he come to regarding the female goats that had four or five kids?

b He correctly calculated that if the probability of twins is $\frac{1}{6}$, then the theoretical probability that a female goat had five kids in four years is 0.3858. Show how he did this calculation.

c Complete the table (over the page) to show the theoretical probabilities that a female goat has 4, 5, 6, 7 or 8 kids in four years if the probability of twins is $\frac{1}{6}$. Use these to calculate the expected numbers of female goats in a flock of 150 that will have 4, 5, 6, 7 or 8 kids.

Number of kids	4	5	6	7	8
Theoretical probability					
Expected numbers					

d Compare the expected number of female goats that will have four or five kids in a flock of 150 (assuming a probability of twins is $\frac{1}{6}$) with the actual numbers in the farmer's flock.

e The number of female goats that had just four kids in four years was 98. Use this value to estimate the actual probability that a female goat in his flock has twins.

f Use this estimate to calculate the number of female goats in his flock that would have five kids in four years.

g Compare your previous answer with the actual number of female goats that had five kids in four years. What conclusion can the farmer come to?

PHOTOCOPYING OF THIS PAGE IS RESTRICTED UNDER LAW. ISBN: 9780170389372

Practice questions

Practice question one

a On a given weekend the people entering a New Zealand zoo were surveyed, and 85% of people were visitors to the zoo, the rest were staff. Of the visitors, 28% had a discount voucher.

Of the visitors who had a voucher:
- 64% were local
- 32% were from the rest of New Zealand
- the rest were overseas visitors.

Of the visitors who didn't have a voucher:
- 23% were local
- 40% were from the rest of New Zealand
- the rest were overseas visitors.

i Calculate the proportion of people who entered the zoo, who were overseas visitors without a voucher.

ii Two consecutive people were randomly selected from those entering the zoo. Calculate the probability that both were staff. Justify any assumptions you have made in this calculation and discuss whether they are reasonable.

b i Mad monkey disease is contracted by 3% of people who visited the zoo. There is a scientific test for mad monkey disease. It is known that the test is not entirely accurate and it returns a false negative 1% of the time (test negative but do have the disease). It also returns a false positive 2% of the time (test positive but don't have the disease).

Calculate the risk that a person does not have the disease, given that they returned a positive test. Explain what this means.

ii Each year, 40,000 people visit the zoo. Some of those who tested positive for mad monkey disease developed a rash due to the test. The probability that a person develops a rash if they have mad monkey disease and test positive is 0.8. The total number of people who developed a rash if they had tested positive for the disease was 1260.

Calculate the probability that a person who had tested positive but didn't have the disease, gets a rash.

PHOTOCOPYING OF THIS PAGE IS RESTRICTED UNDER LAW.
ISBN: 9780170389372

Practice question two

Lemurs are endangered and a special breeding programme is required at the New Zealand zoo to increase numbers. Female lemurs bear one offspring per pregnancy.

Lemurs are expensive to rear so the zoo manager wants as many female lemurs as possible. The manager decides that any female who bears two male offspring will be removed from the breeding programme. All female lemurs are retired from the breeding programme after five offspring.

At the zoo, 60% of newborn baby lemurs are male.

a i Estimate the theoretical probability that a female lemur at the zoo is removed from the breeding programme immediately after her second or third offspring.

ii An overseas zoo has the same policy of removing females from the breeding programme after they bear two male offspring. They have records of the breeding histories for 82 female lemurs.

The table shows the number of offspring females have before they are removed from the breeding programme.

Number of offspring before removal	2	3	4	5
Number of female lemurs	33	30	10	9

Calculate the probability that a female lemur at the overseas zoo is removed from the breeding programme before she has a fourth offspring.

iii What conclusion can the zoo manager make regarding the theoretical probability that a female lemur at his zoo is removed from the breeding programme before she has a fourth offspring, compared with the data from the overseas zoo? Suggest what other relevant information he should seek and why it could be useful.

b i Estimate the theoretical probability that a female lemur is removed from the zoo breeding programme before she has had five offspring.

ii The zoo manager's answer to the previous question was 0.8848, but he was uncertain whether this was correct, so he performed a simulation in order to confirm it. He performed his simulation 40 times, and it showed that 29 females would be removed from the breeding programme before they have had five offspring, and 11 would remain and produce five offspring.

Discuss whether or not he should conclude that his answer to the previous question was incorrect.

PHOTOCOPYING OF THIS PAGE IS RESTRICTED UNDER LAW.
ISBN: 9780170389372

Practice question three

The zoo runs night-time tours to see kiwis. The table shows the percentages of visitors from the North and South Islands who do the night-time tour.

	Did night-time tour	Didn't do night-time tour
North Island	26.7%	29.7%
South Island	19.4%	24.2%

a i Consider the events 'a visitor does the night-time tour' and 'a visitor lives in the South Island'. Explain whether these events are independent.

ii Use your previous answer to discuss the effect of where a visitor lives on whether or not they do the night-time tour. Support your answer with appropriate statistical statements.

b Let the event A be that a visitor does the night-time tour.
Let the event B be that a visitor visited the zoo during the day.
Explain the relationship between these two events if both of the following are true:

$$P(A/B) = 1 \quad \textbf{and} \quad P(B/A) \neq 1$$

c When visitors pay to enter the zoo, they also can buy three different tours: the daytime tour, the night-time tour, and the feeding the animals tour. Records were kept for 1000 visitors to the zoo:

- 425 bought the feeding the animals tour
- 506 bought the daytime tour
- 342 bought the night-time tour
- 384 bought both the feeding the animals and the daytime tour
- 194 bought the feeding the animals and the night-time tour
- 183 bought all three tours
- 401 bought no extra tours.

How many people bought both the daytime and night-time tours, but not the feeding the animals tour?

PHOTOCOPYING OF THIS PAGE IS RESTRICTED UNDER LAW.
ISBN: 9780170389372

Answers

The language of probability (pp. 6–8)

Notation	Highlight the numbers included in the description in the left column:	This could also be written as:
$P(X > 3)$	0 1 2 3 **4 5 6 7 8**	$P(X \geq 4)$
$P(X \leq 2)$	**0 1 2** 3 4 5 6 7 8	$P(X < 3)$
$P(2 < X < 7)$	0 1 2 **3 4 5 6** 7 8	$P(3 \leq X \leq 6)$
$P(X \geq 4)$	0 1 2 3 **4 5 6 7 8**	$P(X > 3)$
$P(X < 3)$	**0 1 2** 3 4 5 6 7 8	$P(X \leq 2)$
$P(X = 1)$	0 **1** 2 3 4 5 6 7 8	$P(0 < X < 2)$
$P(5 \leq X \leq 7)$	0 1 2 3 4 **5 6 7** 8	$P(4 < X < 8)$

Words	Highlight the values that X can take:	Notation(s)
P(*X* is exactly 4)	0 1 2 3 **4** 5 6 7 8	$P(X = 4)$ $P(3 < X < 5)$
P(*X* is greater than 2)	0 1 2 **3 4 5 6 7 8**	$P(X > 2)$ $P(X \geq 3)$
P(*X* is between 3 and 7)	0 1 2 3 **4 5 6** 7 8	$P(3 < X < 7)$ $P(4 \leq X \leq 6)$
P(*X* is less than 5)	**0 1 2 3 4** 5 6 7 8	$P(X < 5)$ $P(X \leq 4)$
P(*X* is at least 6)	0 1 2 3 4 5 **6 7 8**	$P(X \geq 6)$ $P(X > 5)$
P(*X* is between 1 and 4 inclusive)	0 **1 2 3 4** 5 6 7 8	$P(1 \leq X \leq 4)$ $P(0 < X < 5)$
P(*X* is 5 or less)	**0 1 2 3 4 5** 6 7 8	$P(X \leq 5)$ $P(X < 6)$
P(*X* is greater than or equal to 1)	0 **1 2 3 4 5 6 7 8**	$P(X \geq 1)$ $P(X > 0)$
P(*X* is under 7)	**0 1 2 3 4 5 6** 7 8	$P(X < 7)$ $P(X \leq 6)$
P(*X* is over 6)	0 1 2 3 4 5 6 **7 8**	$P(X > 6)$ $P(X \geq 7)$
P(*X* is 2 or more)	0 1 **2 3 4 5 6 7 8**	$P(X \geq 2)$ $P(X > 1)$
P(*X* is more than 5)	0 1 2 3 4 5 **6 7 8**	$P(X > 5)$ $P(X \geq 6)$
P(*X* is not more than 3)	**0 1 2 3** 4 5 6 7 8	$P(X \leq 3)$ $P(X < 4)$
P(*X* exceeds 4)	0 1 2 3 4 **5 6 7 8**	$P(X > 4)$ $P(X \geq 5)$
P(*X* is not less than 7)	0 1 2 3 4 5 6 **7 8**	$P(X \geq 7)$ $P(X > 6)$
P(*X* is less than or equal to 5)	**0 1 2 3 4 5** 6 7 8	$P(X \leq 5)$ $P(X < 6)$
P(*X* is at most 6)	**0 1 2 3 4 5 6** 7 8	$P(X \leq 6)$ $P(X < 7)$

ISBN: 9780170389372 PHOTOCOPYING OF THIS PAGE IS RESTRICTED UNDER LAW.

Probability revision (pp. 9–12)

1 $\frac{1}{7}$ 0.1429 15% 0.181 $\frac{2}{11}$

2 a $\frac{4}{52} = 0.0769$ b $\frac{13}{52} = 0.25$

c $\frac{8}{52} = 0.1538$ d $\frac{12}{52} = 0.2308$

e $\frac{39}{52} = 0.75$ f $\frac{20}{52} = 0.3846$

3 a $\frac{63}{200} = 0.315$ b $\frac{113}{200} = 0.565$

c $\frac{176}{200} = 0.88$ d $\frac{100}{200} = 0.5$

4 a 0.36 b 0.11

c 0.09

5 145

6 125

7 960

8 a 0.1 b 0.125

c 0.5625 d 0.2625

e 0.0142

Multiplication Principle (pp. 14–16)

1 24

2 120

3 6 760 000

4 a 676 b 0.001479

c 0.001538

5 24

6 a 10 000 b 5040

c 9000 d 0.0001

7 a 362 880

b 40 320

c 1440 (Don't forget, the two tallest players can be arranged in two ways.)

8 72

9 3 girls, 4 boys: 14 400 ways

4 girls, 3 boys: 21 600 ways

∴ Total number of ways is 36 000

Methods for displaying probability (pp. 17–48)

Probability and frequency distribution tables and graphs (pp. 17–20)

1 a

No licence	Learner's licence	Restricted licence	Full licence
0.3595	0.4298	0.1736	0.0372

b

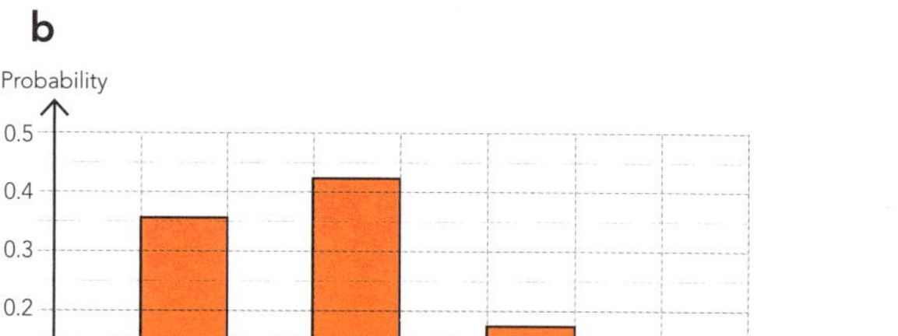

c Method 1: P(licence) = 1 – P(no licence)
= 1 – 0.3595
= 0.6405

P(no licence) = 0.35950 is not rounded.

Method 2: P(licence)
= P(LL) + P(RL) + P(FL)
= 0.4298 + 0.1736 + 0.0372
= 0.6406

All three of these probabilities (0.42975, 0.17355 and 0.03719) have been rounded up, so the sum of these rounding errors accounts for the extra 0.0001.

I would consider the answer from Method 1 to be more accurate because there were no rounding errors.

d

No licence	Learner's licence	Restricted licence	Full licence
0.3388	0.4050	0.2025	0.0537

2 a Missing probability is 0.0682.

b

No licence	Learner's licence	Restricted licence	Full licence
116	178	61	26

c 0.2283

3 a Possible combinations of throws: (6, 4), (5, 4), (2, 2) and (3, 1) – 4 possibilities out of 36.

b

Turns to finish	1	2	> 2
Probability	$\frac{1}{6} = \frac{6}{36}$	$\frac{4}{36}$	$\frac{26}{36}$

4 a

Total value	$T <$ \$1	\$1 $\leq T <$ \$2	$T \geq$ \$2
Probability	$\frac{6}{20} = 0.3$	$\frac{6}{20} = 0.3$	$\frac{8}{20} = 0.4$

PHOTOCOPYING OF THIS PAGE IS RESTRICTED UNDER LAW.
ISBN: 9780170389372

b

Total value	$T < \$1$	$\$1 \le T < \$2$	$T \ge \$2$
Probability	$\frac{8}{25} = 0.32$	$\frac{7}{25} = 0.28$	$\frac{10}{25} = 0.4$

c He should play the game without replacement because the probability of getting more than $1 is 0.70, but if he played it with replacement the probability of getting more than $1 would only be 0.68.

d

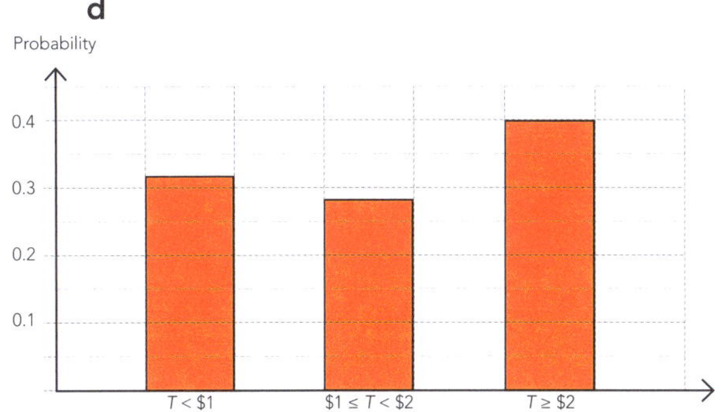

Probabilities with two overlapping groups (pp. 22–27)

1

A B 0.4
0.1 0.3 0.2

	A	A′	
B	0.3	0.2	**0.5**
B′	0.1	0.4	**0.5**
	0.4	**0.6**	**1**

a

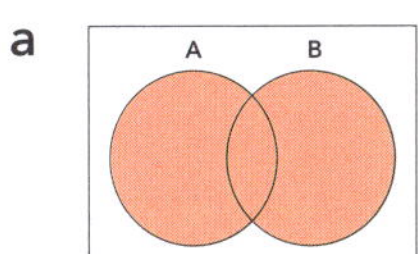

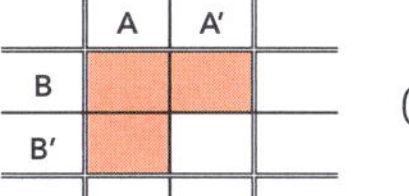

0.6

b

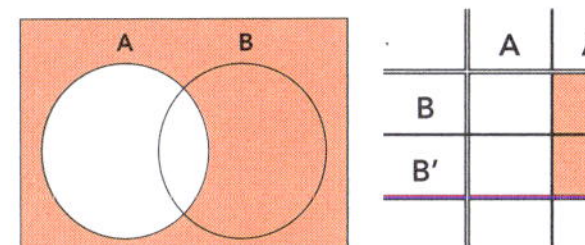

0.6

c

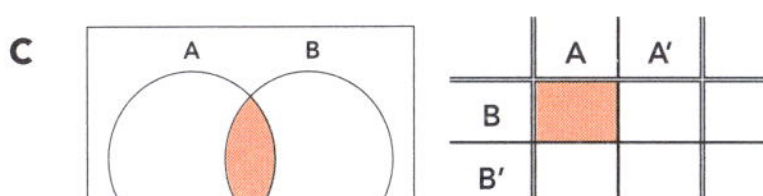

0.3

d

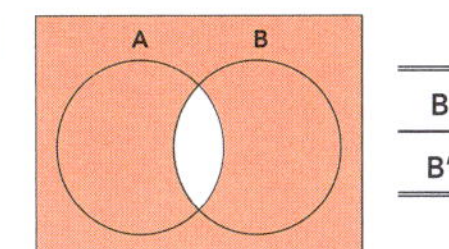

0.7

e

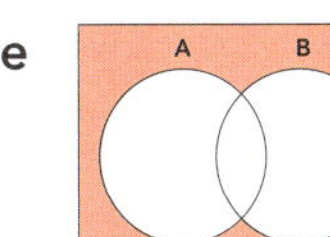

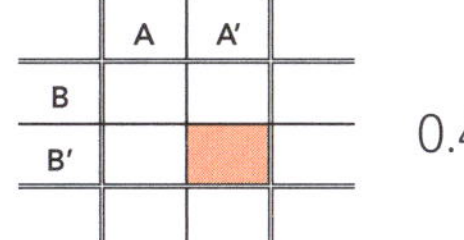

0.4

f

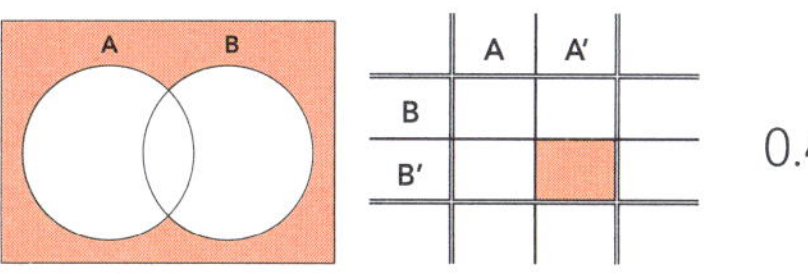

0.4

g

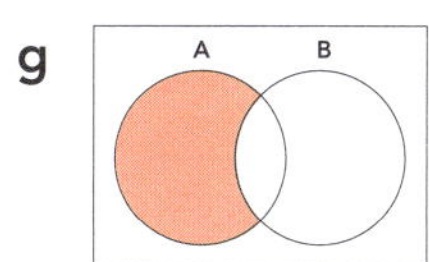

0.1

2

S MI 9
32 5 14

	S	S′	
MI	5	14	**19**
MI′	32	9	**41**
	37	**23**	**60**

a

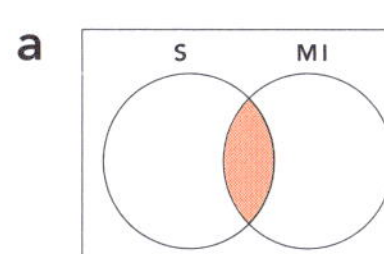

$\frac{5}{60} = 0.08\dot{3}$

b

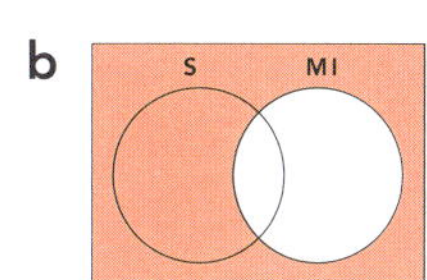

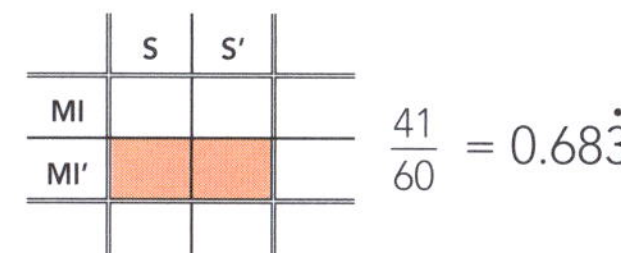

$\frac{41}{60} = 0.68\dot{3}$

c

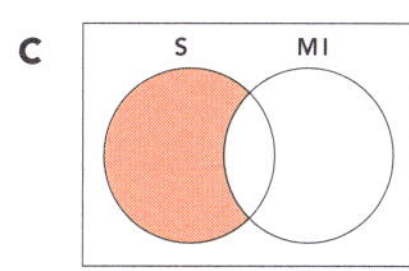

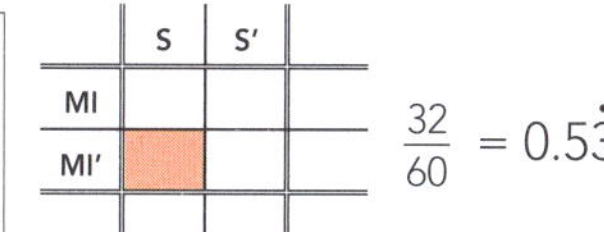

$\frac{32}{60} = 0.5\dot{3}$

d

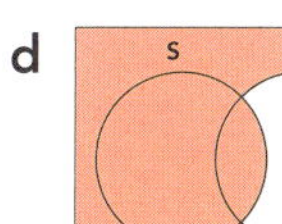
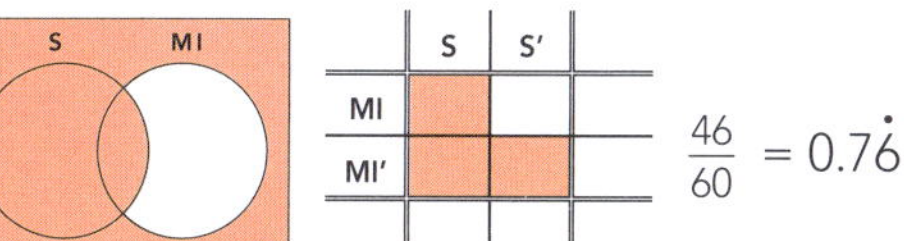

$\frac{46}{60} = 0.7\dot{6}$

e

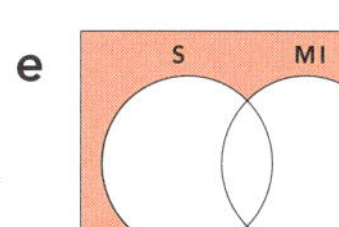

$\frac{9}{60} = 0.15$

f

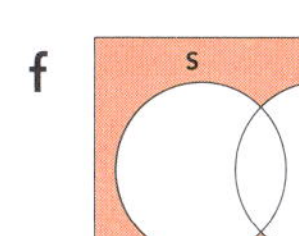

$\frac{9}{60} = 0.15$

g

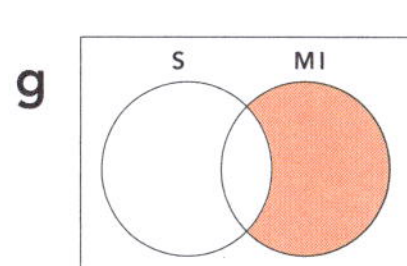

$\frac{14}{60} = 0.2\dot{3}$

3

	B	B′	
M	3	25	**28**
M′	12	40	**52**
	15	**65**	**80**

$P = \frac{12}{80} = 0.15$

ISBN: 9780170389372 PHOTOCOPYING OF THIS PAGE IS RESTRICTED UNDER LAW.

4 a

	ON	ON′	
TB	7	21	**28**
TB′	55	17	**72**
	62	**38**	**100**

P = 17%

b $P = \frac{7}{62} = 0.1129$

c $P = \frac{21}{38} = 0.5526$

5 a 0.09

b $P = \frac{22}{28} = 0.7857$

c $P = \frac{22}{31} = 0.7097$

6 a 82

b Males: $P = \frac{22}{58} = 0.3793$

Females: $P = \frac{16}{62} = 0.2581$

∴ Males were more likely than females to cycle the track.

7 40

Challenge: 14 people.

Probabilities with three overlapping groups (pp. 28–35)

1 a

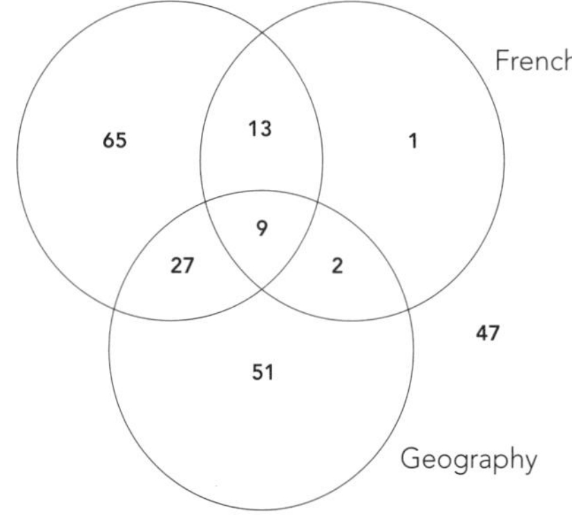

b 47

c $\frac{13 + 2 + 27}{215} = 0.1953$

2 a

		One News	*Not One News*	TOTALS
Shortland Street	*The Bachelor*	1	14	22
	Not The Bachelor	0	7	
Not Shortland Street	*The Bachelor*	3	24	78
	Not The Bachelor	5	46	
TOTALS		9	91	100

b 15

c $\frac{5 + 3 + 1}{100} = 0.09$

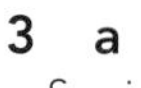

3 a

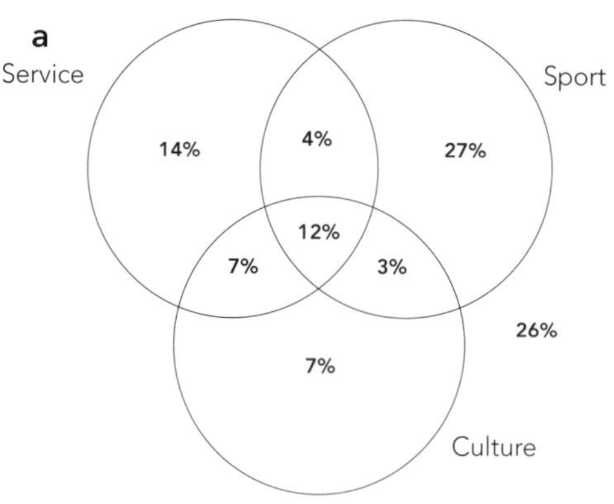

		Sport	Not Sport	TOTALS
Service	Culture	12	7	37
	Not Culture	4	14	
Not Service	Culture	3	7	63
	Not Culture	27	26	
TOTALS		46	54	100

b 28%

c $\frac{15}{46} = 32.61\%$

4 a

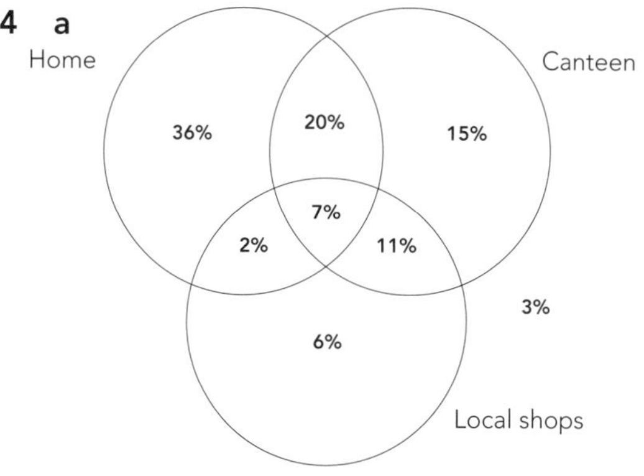

		Canteen	Not Canteen	TOTALS
Home	Local shops	7	2	65
	Not Local shops	20	36	
Not Home	Local shops	11	6	35
	Not Local shops	15	3	
TOTALS		53	47	100

b 26%

c $\frac{18}{26} = 0.6923$

PHOTOCOPYING OF THIS PAGE IS RESTRICTED UNDER LAW.
ISBN: 9780170389372

5 a

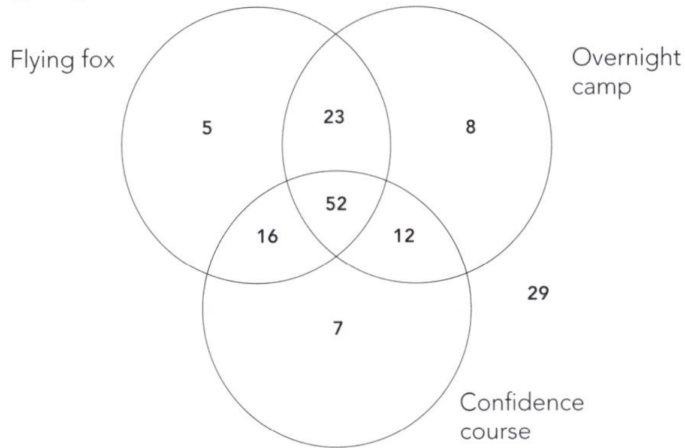

		Confidence course	Not Confidence course	TOTALS
Flying fox	Overnight camp	52	23	96
	Not Overnight camp	16	5	
Not Flying fox	Overnight camp	12	8	56
	Not Overnight camp	7	29	
TOTALS		87	65	152

b 52

c $\frac{52 + 16}{96} = 0.7083$

6 a

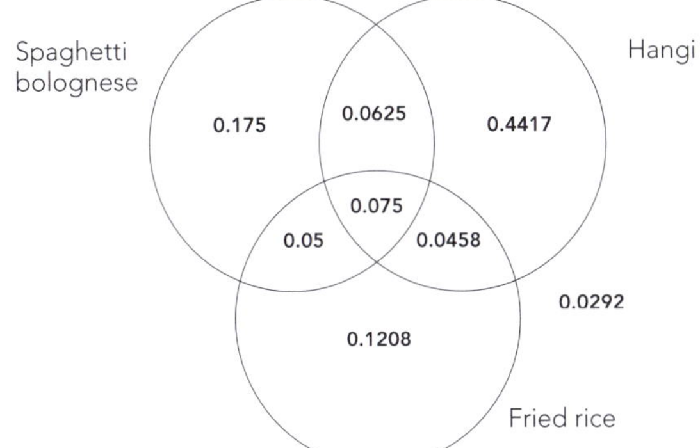

		Spaghetti bolognese	Not Spaghetti bolognese	TOTALS
Hangi	Fried rice	0.075	0.0458	0.625
	Not Fried rice	0.0625	0.4417	
Not Hangi	Fried rice	0.05	0.1208	0.375
	Not Fried rice	0.175	0.0292	
TOTALS		0.3625	0.6375	1

b 0.075

Probabilities from tables of counts (pp. 36–39)

1 **a** 0.0841 **b** 0.3042
c 0.3172 **d** 0.7767
e 0.1845 **f** 0.8511
g 0.1163

2 **a** 0.166 **b** 0.04
c 0.022 **d** 0.808
e 0.85 **f** 0.8549
g 0.4459

3 **a** 0.1526 **b** 0.3852
c 0.3401 **d** 0.3989
e 0.6577 **f** 0.9100
g 0.6243

Probability trees (pp. 40–48)

1 a

b 0.3016
c 0.4264
d 87.52%
e 38.08%
f

	S	S′	
G	0.2184	0.3016	**0.52**
B	0.3552	0.1248	**0.48**
	0.5736	**0.4264**	1

2 **a** $0.08\dot{3}$
b $0.\dot{5}$
c

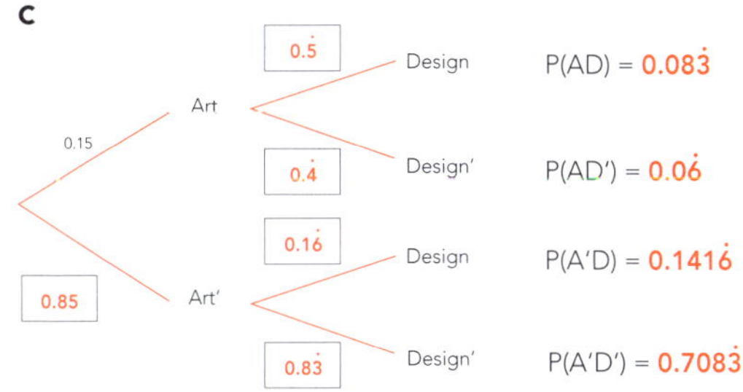

d

	D	D′	
A	$0.08\dot{3}$	$0.0\dot{6}$	**0.15**
A′	$0.141\dot{6}$	$0.708\dot{3}$	**0.85**
	0.2250	**0.7750**	1

ISBN: 9780170389372
PHOTOCOPYING OF THIS PAGE IS RESTRICTED UNDER LAW.

e 0.2083

f $0.1\dot{6}$

g 0.0860

h $\frac{170}{240} \times \frac{169}{239} = 0.5009$

3 a

A 0.7: B 0.9, B' 0.1; A' 0.3: B 0.85, B' 0.15

P(AB) = 0.63

P(AB') = 0.07

P(A'B) = 0.255

P(A'B') = 0.045

b 0.325

c 0.7119

4 a

A 0.9: B 0.4, B' 0.6; A' 0.1: B 0.2, B' 0.8

P(AB) = 0.36

P(AB') = 0.54

P(A'B) = 0.02

P(A'B') = 0.08

b 0.38

c 0.8710

d Amy is more than twice as likely to do the skydive than Ben, but if she does it, then Ben is twice as likely to do it. It is very likely that Amy will skydive.

5 a

NZ 0.310: J 0.271, J' 0.729; O 0.690: J 0.813, J' 0.187

P(NZJ) = 0.084

P(NZJ') = 0.226

P(OJ) = 0.561

P(OJ') = 0.129

b 0.084

c 0.271

d 0.870

e 0.813

f 0.3147

g Just under one third of their clients are New Zealanders and just over two thirds are from overseas. Overseas visitors are three times more likely to go jet-boating than New Zealanders.

6 a

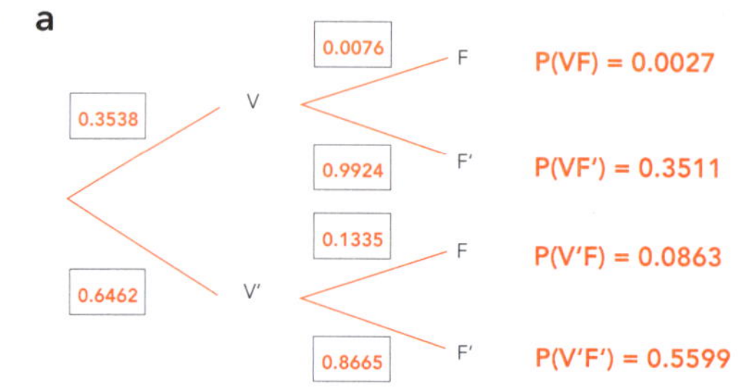

b 0.089

c 0.9697

d 0.1335

e 0.0076

f 0.0606

g About 35% of mothers were vaccinated against the flu. Unvaccinated babies were more than 17 times ($\frac{0.1335}{0.0076}$) more likely to get the flu than unvaccinated babies.

7 a

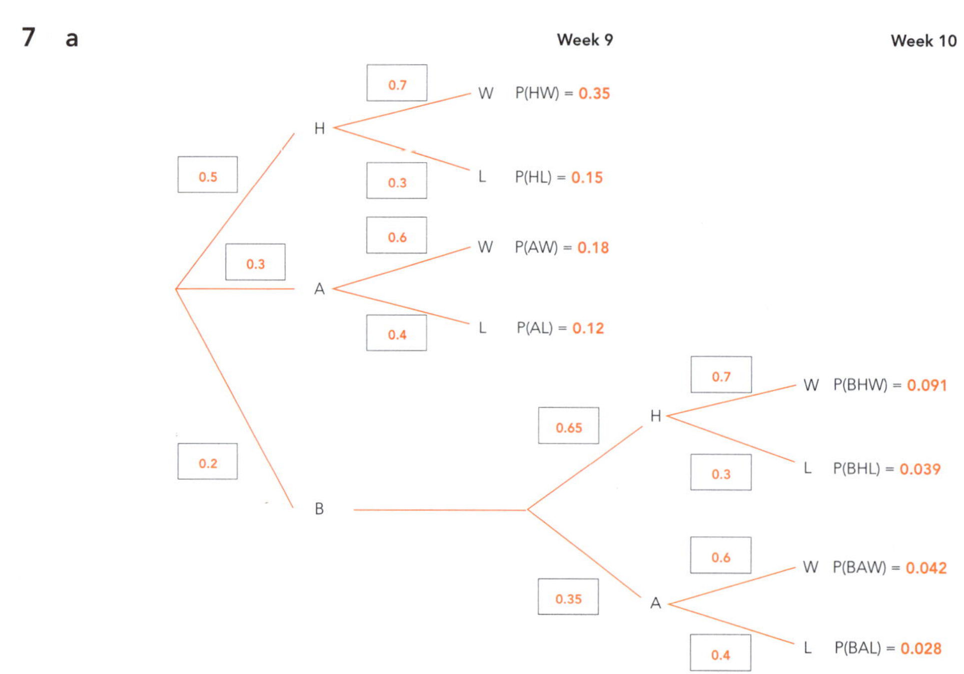

PHOTOCOPYING OF THIS PAGE IS RESTRICTED UNDER LAW.

ISBN: 9780170389372

b 0.663
c 0.7994
d 0.133

8 **a**

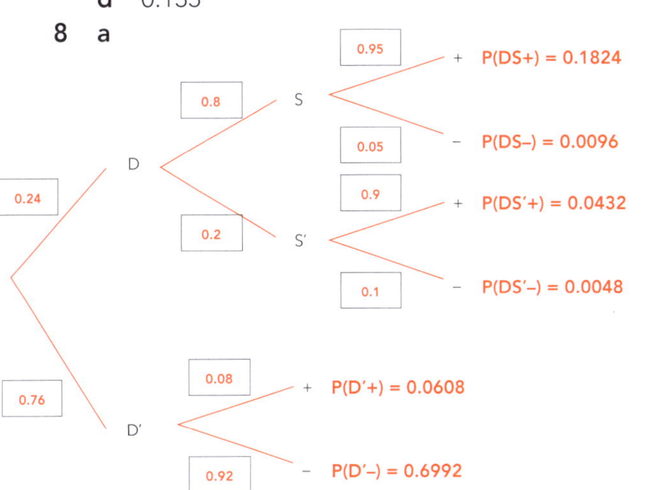

b 0.2864
c 78.77%
d 2.018 %
e 0.2551

Interrelationships between events (pp. 49–64)

Putting it together (pp. 55–58)

1

		P(A/B) or P(B/A)?
a	The probability that a student is a boy given that the student has a pink phone.	P(B/A)
b	The probability that the student has a pink phone if the student is a boy.	P(A/B)
c	The probability that a boy owns a pink phone.	P(A/B)
d	The probability that a student is a boy if he owns a pink phone.	P(B/A)
e	The probability that a student owns a pink phone, given that the student is a boy.	P(A/B)
f	The probability that a pink phone owner is a boy.	P(B/A)

2 **a** 0.6 **b** 0.375
3 **a** 0.2 **b** $0.\dot{3}$
4 **a** 0.55 **b** $0.\dot{5}\dot{4}$
5 **a** 0.5 **b** $0.\dot{6}$
c 0.7
6 **a** 0.5 **b** 0.4
c 0.2

7 **a**

	A	A′	
B	0.28	0.12	**0.4**
B′	0.42	0.18	**0.6**
	0.7	**0.3**	**1**

b No, because P(A ∩ B) = 0.28, which is not equal to 0.
c 0.42
d 0.7

8 **a**

	A	A′	
B	0	0.45	**0.45**
B′	0.2	0.35	**0.55**
	0.2	**0.8**	**1**

b Yes, because P(A ∩ B) = 0.
c 0.2
d 1
e All of B lies with A′; if B occurs, then so must A′. (Drawing a Venn diagram would help to explain this.)

9 **a**

	A	A′	
B	0.1	0.6	**0.7**
B′	0.25	0.05	**0.3**
	0.35	**0.65**	**1**

b No, because P(A ∩ B) = 0.1, which is not equal to 0.
c 0.6
d 0.1429

10 **a**

	S	S′	
F	0.05	0.84	**0.89**
F′	0.07	0.04	**0.11**
	0.12	**0.88**	**1**

b No, because P(A ∩ B) = 0.05, and this is not equal to 0.
c 0.0562
d $0.41\dot{6}$

11 **a**

b 0.9212

ISBN: 9780170389372
PHOTOCOPYING OF THIS PAGE IS RESTRICTED UNDER LAW.

Independent events (pp. 59–64)

1 **a** No: $P(A) \times P(B) = 0.4 \times 0.3 = 0.12$
$P(A \cap B) = 0.2$
$\therefore P(A) \times P(B) \neq P(A \cap B)$

b No: $P(A) = 0.2$
$P(A/B) = 0.3$
$\therefore P(A) \neq P(A/B)$

c Yes: $P(A) \times P(B) = 0.5 \times 0.2 = 0.11$
$P(A \cap B) = 0.1$
$\therefore P(A) \times P(B) = P(A \cap B)$

d Yes: $P(B) = 0.45$
$P(B/A) = 0.45$
$\therefore P(B) = P(B/A)$

2 **a** Yes: Possible answers:

1 $P(A) = 0.3$
$P(A/B) = 0.3$
$\therefore P(A) = P(A/B)$

2 $P(A) \times P(B) = 0.2 \times 0.3 = 0.06$
$P(A \cap B) = 0.06$
$\therefore P(A) \times P(B) = P(A \cap B)$

b No: Possible answers:

1 $P(A) = 0.6$
$P(A/B) = 0.5$
$\therefore P(A) \neq P(A/B)$

2 $P(A) \times P(B) = 0.6 \times 0.8 = 0.48$
$P(A \cap B) = 0.4$
$\therefore P(A) \times P(B) \neq P(A \cap B)$

c Yes: Possible answers:

1 $P(A) = 0.6$
$P(A/B) = 0.6$
$\therefore P(A) = P(A/B)$

2 $P(A) \times P(B) = 0.6 \times 0.75 = 0.45$
$P(A \cap B) = 0.45$
$\therefore P(A) \times P(B) = P(A \cap B)$

3 **a**

	A	**A′**	
B	0.42	0.28	**0.7**
B′	0.18	0.12	**0.3**
	0.6	**0.4**	**1**

b 0.88
c 0.7

4 **a**

	E	**E′**	
S	0.14	0.26	**0.4**
S′	0.21	0.39	**0.6**
	0.35	**0.65**	**1**

b 0.61
c 0.4

5 **a** 0.11

b No: Possible answers:

1 $P(E) = 0.5$
$P(E/H) = 0.7\dot{3}$
$\therefore P(E) \neq P(E/H)$

2 $P(E) \times P(H) = 0.35 \times 0.15 = 0.0525$
$P(E \cap H) = 0.11$
$\therefore P(E) \times P(H) \neq P(E \cap H)$

6 **a** 0.2367
b 0.9668
c No: Possible answers:

1 $P(S) = 0.211$
$P(S/D) = 0.2367$
$\therefore P(S) \neq P(S/D)$

2 $P(D) = 0.862$
$P(D/S) = 0.9668$
$\therefore P(D) \neq P(D/S)$

3 $P(S) \times P(D) = 0.211 \times 0.862 = 0.1819$
$P(S \cap D) = 0.204$
$\therefore P(S) \times P(D) \neq P(S \cap D)$

d **1** Because $P(S/D) > P(S)$, people are more likely than expected to smoke if they drink alcohol.

2 Because $P(D/S) > P(D)$, people are more likely than expected to drink alcohol if they smoke.

3 Because $P(S \cap D) > P(S) \times P(D)$, people are more likely than expected to both smoke and drink.

7 **a** No: Possible answers:

1 $P(N) = 0.204$
$P(N/< 40) = 0.0798$
$\therefore P(N) \neq P(N/< 40)$

2 $P(N) \times P(< 40) = 0.204 \times 0.677 = 0.1381$
$P(N \cap < 40) = 0.0538$
$\therefore P(N) \times P(< 40) \neq P(N \cap < 40)$

b **1** Because $P(N/< 40) < P(N)$, customers who are under 40 years old are less likely than expected to buy a newspaper.

2 Because $P(N \cap < 40) < P(N) \times P(< 40)$, fewer customers than expected were both under 40 years old and bought a newspaper.

8 **a** 0.225
b 0.7963
c 0.5
d No: Possible answers:

1 $P(A) = 0.2986$
$P(A/R) = 0.3933$
$\therefore P(A) \neq P(A/R)$

2 $P(A) \times P(R) = 0.2986 \times 0.4218 = 0.1259$
$P(A \cap R) = 0.1659$
$\therefore P(A) \times P(R) \neq P(A \cap R)$

PHOTOCOPYING OF THIS PAGE IS RESTRICTED UNDER LAW.
ISBN: 9780170389372

e **1** Because P(A/R) > P(A), cars that sold in fewer than 20 days were more likely than expected to be sold for less than $10 000.

2 Because P(A ∩ R) > P(A) x P(R), cars were more likely than expected to both sell for less than $10 000 and be sold in fewer than 20 days.

f Theoretically, the events are not independent because P(A) ≠ P(A/S) and P(A) x P(S) ≠ P(A ∩ S). However, their values are very close, so effectively these events are independent.

Possible answers:

1 P(A) = 0.2986
P(A/S) = 0.3012
∴ P(A) ≅ P(A/S)

2 P(A) x P(S) = 0.2986 x 0.3934 = 0.1175
P(A ∩ S) = 0.1185
∴ P(A) x P(S) ≅ P(A ∩ S)

g **1** Because P(A ∩ R) ≅ P(A), the fact that a car sold in fewer than 20 days made almost no difference to the probability it sold for less than $10 000.

2 Because P(A ∩ R) ≅ P(A) x P(R), cars were not more likely than expected to both sell for less than $10 000 and be sold in fewer than 20 days.

Risk (pp. 65–72)

1 **a**

	Multiple births	Single births	Totals
Extra feed	137	263	400
No extra feed	46	204	250
Totals	183	467	650

b 0.2815 **c** 0.3425

d 0.184 **e** 1.861

f Ewes that were fed extra were 1.861 times as likely to have multiple births compared with ewes that did not get extra feed.

g The weather will vary from year to year, and that may affect the probability of a ewe having multiple births; particularly rainfall, as this will affect the amount of feed.

Whether or not the same rams were used the following year, because some rams may be more likely to produce multiple births in ewes.

The farmer should consider the ages of the ewes, because age might affect the likelihood of multiple births.

2 **a**

	Lung cancer	No lung cancer	Totals
Smokers	220	180	400
Non-smokers	32	568	600
Totals	252	748	1000

b 0.252

c 0.55

d 0.0533

e 10.31

f It means that smokers are more than 10 times as likely to develop lung cancer, compared with non-smokers.

g You would expect 126 to have lung cancer.

Finding 132 people with lung cancer may be due to chance, because a difference of 6 is not very many out of 400 or 500. It produces an absolute risk of having lung cancer of 0.264, which is higher than 0.252.

However, this could also be due to other factors that might influence the incidence of lung cancer in the other study. For example, air pollution, ethnicity, passive smoking, ages, and likely occupations of people in the second study compared with those in the original area.

3 **a**

	Heart attack	No heart attack	Totals
Aspirin	135	9865	10 000
Placebo	175	7825	8 000
Totals	310	17 690	18 000

b $0.017\dot{2}$

c 0.0135

d 0.0219

e 0.6171

f A person who takes aspirin is 0.6171 as likely to have a heart attack, compared with a person who takes a placebo.

ISBN: 9780170389372 PHOTOCOPYING OF THIS PAGE IS RESTRICTED UNDER LAW.

g Whether the ages and genders of the people in the two groups are similar. Also whether there are big differences in life styles (active versus sedentary), exercise regimes, and weights of people in the two groups, because people who are overweight or inactive are probably more likely to have heart attacks.

4 a

	Ate chicken	Did not eat chicken	Totals
Ill	172	12	**184**
Not ill	104	92	**196**
Totals	**276**	**104**	**380**

b 0.4842
c 0.6232
d 0.1154
e 5.4
f A student who had eaten chicken was 5.4 times as likely to be ill, compared with a student who did not eat chicken.
g 225 people. If 143 were ill, that represents an absolute risk of being ill of 0.3075, which is a lot lower than the value of 0.4842 at the first formal, and probably not just due to chance. However, I would not be surprised many other factors could have been involved. The chicken may not have been heated properly at the first formal, or it may not have been stored in the fridge. It may be that fewer people ate the chicken at the second formal.

5 a 2013: Risk = 0.0483
2014: Risk = 0.0570
2015: Risk = 0.0610
∴ Risk was greatest during 2015.
b The risk is 1.263 times as great in 2015.
c Some of the people who were driving in the area and got tickets may not live in the area. There will probably be some people driving in the area who do not have licences.
d It may not be very accurate due to chance — it may just happen that more or fewer drivers are caught speeding. The traffic department may alter its policing regime in 2016 — for instance they may have a blitz on speeding, or install speed cameras. It's easier to speed on some types of roads, so if roads have been altered, then more or fewer people might speed.

6 a 6.948
b It means that it is about seven times as risky to travel a particular distance in a car, compared with travelling the same distance on a commercial flight.
c The number of people killed per kilometre while travelling in car is likely to be reasonably stable. The number could change a little due to such factors as altered traffic policing, improvements in roads and better safety standards of cars. The number of people killed while travelling on a commercial flight is likely to vary widely from year to year. Commercial flights usually carry lots of people at once, and just one accident in a year could result in a much higher risk of being killed.

7 a 0.0868
b Only 8.68% of those who test positive will actually have the disease.
c 0.9999
d If you test negative for this condition, it is almost certain that you do not have it.

Simulation (pp. 75–80)

1 a $\frac{1}{9}$
b His conclusion was not valid because he did not perform the simulation enough times. With nine different possibilities, the expected frequency for each digit is $5.\dot{5}$, but because this number is small, there is likely to be a lot of variation in the frequencies.
c Because the simulation was done 1000 times, her results are likely to reflect true probabilities. They suggest that all digits are equally likely as leading digits for populations.
d

Number	1	2	3	4	5	6	7	8	9
Frequency	70	32	25	23	15	12	7	9	7
Probability	0.35	0.16	0.125	0.115	0.075	0.06	0.035	0.045	0.035

e The assumption was incorrect: 1 is the most frequent leading digit, then the probabilities of each digit leading decrease through to a lowest probability for 9. The decrease is not linear, but exponential — the biggest drop is

PHOTOCOPYING OF THIS PAGE IS RESTRICTED UNDER LAW.
ISBN: 9780170389372

between 1 and 2, next biggest between 2 and 3, etc.

2 a i Yes. In theory they have removed one card from the pool of cards in New Zealand each time they buy a packet of cereal, so the probability of drawing another card the same should be reduced. However, because there will be such a large number of packets, the probability of drawing the same card again will be reduced only very slightly, so the probability of getting any particular card remains close to 0.25. If they removed a card, the probability of getting the same card twice would reduce from $\frac{4}{16}$ (0.25) to $\frac{3}{16}$ (0.1875).

ii

Number of cards → full set	4	5	6	> 6
Frequency	3	6	5	16
Probability	0.1	0.2	$0.1\dot{6}$	$0.5\dot{3}$

iii

Number of cards → full set	4	5	6	> 6
Frequency	94	142	147	617
Probability	0.094	0.142	0.147	0.617

iv No, he is not correct. The simulation shows that the probability of completing the set by buying six packets, or fewer, of cereal is 0.383, which is significantly less than 0.5. Because the simulation was repeated 1000 times, this probability is likely to be close to the true probability.

b P(4 different cards) = $1 \times \frac{3}{4} \times \frac{2}{4} \times \frac{1}{4} = \frac{6}{64}$ = 0.0938 (4 dp)

c Ways this can happen:

Second card the same as the first:
$1 \times \frac{1}{4} \times \frac{3}{4} \times \frac{2}{4} \times \frac{1}{4} = \frac{6}{256}$

Third card the same as the first or second:
$1 \times \frac{3}{4} \times \frac{2}{4} \times \frac{2}{4} \times \frac{1}{4} = \frac{12}{256}$

Fourth card the same as the first, second or third: $1 \times \frac{3}{4} \times \frac{2}{4} \times \frac{3}{4} \times \frac{1}{4} = \frac{18}{256}$

∴ Total probability of getting the complete set after five packets
$= \frac{36}{256} = 0.1406$ (4 dp)

d

Number of cards → full set	4	5	6	> 6
Probability	0.0938	0.1406	0.1465	0.6191

e They could trade cards or give each other their duplicate cards.

f That the cereal company has not really put equal numbers of each card into packets. If they made one particular card far less common, it might have the effect of making people buy more cereal in order to get a complete set.

3 a For the female goats that had four kids:
For his flock, P(4) = $\frac{98}{150} = 0.65\dot{3}$
From the simulation, P (4) = 0.485
There is a large difference between these values, which suggests that P(twins) $\neq \frac{1}{6}$.
Because the probability of having four kids (no twins) is much higher for his flock, it is likely that the probability of twins is much lower than $\frac{1}{6}$.
For the female goats that had five kids:
For his flock, P(5) = $\frac{44}{150} = 0.29\dot{3}$
From the simulation, P (4) = 0.384
There is a large difference between these values, which once again suggests that P(twins) $\neq \frac{1}{6}$.
Because the probability of having five kids (one set of twins) is lower for his flock, once again this suggests that the probability of twins is lower than $\frac{1}{6}$.

b P(5 kids) = $4 \times \left(\frac{1}{6}\right)^1 \times \left(\frac{5}{6}\right)^3 = 0.3858$

c

Number of kids	4	5	6	7	8
Theoretical probability	0.4823	0.3858	0.1157	0.0154	0.0008
Expected numbers	72	58	17	2	0

Due to rounding errors, this comes to 149, so you could expect one more in one of these columns.

d For the female goats that had four kids: the expected number is 72, but the actual number was 98. Once again, this strongly suggests that the probability of twins is much lower than $\frac{1}{6}$ because far more goats than expected had no twins.
For the female goats that had five kids: the expected number is 58, but the actual number was 44. Once again, this strongly suggests that the probability of twins is much lower than $\frac{1}{6}$ because fewer goats than expected had a set of twins.

e Let p = probability of a single birth.
$p^4 = \frac{98}{150}$ so $p = 0.8990$
∴ Estimate that the probability that a female goat has a single kid = 0.9, so P(twins) = 0.1.

f P(5 kids) = $4 \times (0.1)^1 \times (0.9)^3 = 0.2913$
∴ Expected number of females that would have 5 kids is 0.2916 x 150 = 44

g Because the estimated number of female goats having five kids in four years is the same as the actual number, it is very likely that the probability of twins is about 0.1, and not $0.1\dot{6}$ or $\frac{1}{6}$ as he had been promised.

Practice questions (pp. 81–86)

Practice question one (pp. 81–82)

a i P(visitor ∩ no voucher ∩ international)
= 0.2264

ii P(both staff) = $0.15^2 = 0.0255$
The assumption is that of independence: that the first person is a staff member does not affect the probability that the second person is a staff member.
It is likely they are not independent as staff would tend to enter together because they travel together or arrive on the same bus. They would also tend to arrive at certain times of the day, e.g. in the morning or evening.

b i P(doesn't have disease/positive test)
= 0.02 x 0.97/(0.0297+0.0194) = 0.3951
39.51% of those who test positive don't actually have the disease.

ii Number who are D and + and R =
P(D ∩ + ∩ R) x 40 000 = 0.03 x 0.99 x 0.8 x 40 000 = 950
Number who are D′ and + and R = 1260 – 950 = 310
Number who are D′ and + = .97 x .02 x 40 000 = 776
∴ Probability of getting rash/(D′ and +)
= 310/776 = 0.3995

Practice question two (pp. 83–84)

a i Second: P(BB) = $0.6^2 = 0.36$
P(GBB or BGB) = $0.4 \times 0.6^2 \times 2 = 0.288$
Total = 0.648

ii P(removed at overseas zoo) = $\frac{63}{82} = 0.7683$

iii This suggests that the breeding programme at the New Zealand zoo is more successful than the overseas zoo, because fewer lemurs are removed from the programme by the time they have three offspring.
He should find out whether:

- the probability that a newborn lemur is a male is also 0.6 at the overseas zoo
- other factors such as what they are fed and climatic conditions are similar
- the probability that a newborn lemur is a male remains at 0.6 throughout the life of the mother.

b i P(BB) = $0.6^2 = 0.36$
P(BGB or GBB) = 0.288
P(GBGB or GGBB or BGGB) = $0.4^2 \times 0.6^2 \times 3 = 0.1728$
Total = 0.36 + 0.288 + 0.1728 = 0.8208

ii 29/40 = 0.725, which is considerably less than 0.8848.
This makes it likely that his answer was wrong. However, he only did his simulation 40 times, which is a relatively small number, so he may by chance have got fewer than the 35/40 that he could expect if his answer were correct. He could be more certain if he performed his simulation many more times.

Practice question three (pp. 85–86)

a i P(night-time tour) x P(South Island) =
0.461 x 0.436 = 0.201
P(night-time tour and South Island) = 0.194
$0.201 \neq 0.194$
Therefore not independent.

Or P(South Island/night-time tour) =
P(South Island and night-time tour)/
P(night-time tour)
$= \frac{0.194}{0.461} = 0.4208$
P(South Island) = $0.436 \neq 0.4208$
Therefore not independent.

Or P(night-time tour/South Island) =
P(South Island and night-time tour)/
P(South Island)
$= \frac{0.194}{0.436} = 0.445$
P(night-time tour) = $0.461 \neq 0.445$
Therefore not independent.

PHOTOCOPYING OF THIS PAGE IS RESTRICTED UNDER LAW.
ISBN: 9780170389372

However, while the final values in each calculation are different, they are not very different, e.g. 0.461 is close to 0.445. This means that the event 'a visitor bought a night-time tour' and the event 'a visitor was from the South Island' are almost independent. In other words, being from the South Island makes very little difference to whether a visitor does the night-time tour or not.

ii P(night-time tour/South Island) = P(South Island and night-time tour)/P(South Island)

$= \frac{0.194}{0.463} = 0.4450$

P(night-time tour/North Island) = P(North Island and night-time tour)/P(North Island)

$= \frac{0.267}{0.564} = 0.4734$

Therefore students in the South Island are slightly less likely to do the night-time tour.

Or

Therefore students in the North Island are slightly more likely to do the night-time tour.

However, there is not a huge difference in these answers, so where a visitor lives does not have a major effect on whether or not they do the night-time tour.

b All those who did the night-time tour also visited the zoo during the day.

But not everybody who visited the zoo during the day did the night-time tour.

c

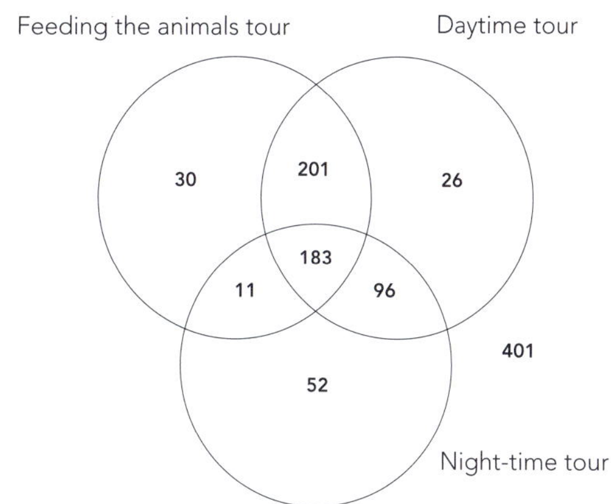

96 people

Removable section

Word	Definition	Example problems	Answer
Experimental probability	2	B	0.958
Theoretical probability	8	E	$0.19\dot{4}$
Multiplication Principle	1	G	$0.0\dot{6}$
Intersection	6	J	0.05
Disjoint events	3	A	0
Complementary events	7	F	0
Conditional probability	5	H	0.2
Independent event	9	C	0.25
Absolute risk	10	D	0.1975
Relative risk	4	I	8.49

 PHOTOCOPYING OF THIS PAGE IS RESTRICTED UNDER LAW.